DARING

DARING

Vesna Zuvic

authorHOUSE®

AuthorHouse™
1663 Liberty Drive
Bloomington, IN 47403
www.authorhouse.com
Phone: 1-800-839-8640

Published by AuthorHouse   10/16/2012

ISBN: 978-1-4772-3921-6 (sc)
ISBN: 978-1-4772-3922-3 (e)

This book is dedicated to our children: Frane, Mario, Sara, and Alan

"I say to my child, I will explain to you as much of life as I can, but you must remember that there is a part of life for which you are the explanation."

—Robert Brault

Acknowledgments

I would like to thank all those who have generously walked along with me, only to encourage me to explore and unleash the deep abysses of my hidden self.

Special thanks to:

My parents, because they had the courage to let me go find myself outside the limits of their reach.

My sisters—Maria, Svetka, and Anka; and Mario, my brother—because they loved me even when they could not understand me.

My friend—Tamara . . . because she was a pillar of support when I needed one most.

Our children—Frane, Alan, Mario, and Sara—for they have touched and continue to touch my heart in a way that only children can—with love, honesty, and joy.

Sead, who has unconditionally loved, encouraged, and supported me through the last ten years of our life.

In loving memory of my adopted mother, Maria, for she had accepted me as her own.

Dear Reader,

Have you ever asked yourself—what is the purpose of life? What is the meaning of *my* life? Why do things happen the way they do? Why me?

If so, then you may be able to relate to my story and perhaps find an answer for yourself too. The contents of this book are personal yet relatable to anybody's story of hardship and triumph. My intention is not to judge or preach. The writing has emerged entirely from a personal need for expression and healing and as a final point in a period of my life which has come to an end for me. It is not meant to be the absolute truth, just a personal testimony about a fraction of time undertaken on this endless journey of life. If it encourages you while reading or prompts you into acting—as it has freed me while writing—then it is safe to say it has served its purpose well.

The book is divided into three parts, each beginning with some personally significant memories from my life, concluding with lessons I've learned along the way. Part one, *In Search of a Time Lost: The Early Years,* covers my early childhood and the impact it had on the following years. *To Love Is to Change: Light at the End of the Corridor* sums up my more mature years and brings to light the changes that have happened within. Part three, *The Path of the Heart,* summarizes my life's teachings so far with a recollection of thoughts that have emerged along the way.

> *"Our own private intuition is the catalyst for self-improvement and self-realization, because when it comes to making deep and lasting changes in one's personal life, it is only subjective experience, not facts, that registers as real."*

> **—Penney Peirce**

Prologue

"Do not believe in anything simply because you have heard it . . .

Do not believe in anything simply because it is spoken and rumored by many . . .

Do not believe in anything simply because it is found written in your religious books . . .

Do not believe in anything merely on the authority of your teachers and elders . . .

Do not believe in traditions because they have been handed down for many generations . . .

But after observation and analysis, when you find that anything agrees with reason and is conducive to the good and benefit of one and all, then accept it and live up to it."

—Buddha

Have you ever found yourself in a situation where the ground seems to crumble beneath your feet because of the intensity and flurry of the force within? The world as you know it collapses and collides, but still you stand, peaceful and strong in the moment of recognition that you are safe, protected, and loved. Both birth and death appear simultaneously, peace and chaos, the creation and disintegration—and everything seems perfect in its sense of existence. By stepping into the unknown, my final quest for meaning has begun, inevitable and doubtless, because one can no longer return to the reality of the foreseen. Predestination and programming, rationalization and the need to control, the race to achieve goals—it all loses significance in the light of what I have just discovered. The seemingly chaotic environment emerges in peace, and I discover that it has always been there, hidden under layers of fear, enveloped in a feeling of inadequacy and guilt, bathed in an atmosphere of a time past.

It seems as though the search of forty-four years has been infinitely long. A flash of defeat illuminates the mind of one who is just getting used to letting go. I did so much wandering and roaming around in circles, searching for myself in places where I did not exist and the realization that I just had to remember: we are more than transience in the midst of notorious reality. We are of this world equally—the body and spirit in one—connected in an extraordinary dance with everything that surrounds us in infinity. Where dark resided before, a magnificent light emerges in faith, and the sensation that has for so long consumed my body relaxes and loosens in the force that summons in its mystical lucidity. I do not know what draws me to it, but all resistance is inefficient. I cannot recede while my inner sense suggests taking the path unknown. Nevertheless, I do not fear, while boldly stepping out into the darkness once again, adjusting momentarily to obscurity at hand, I feel peaceful in the knowledge of being on to something more than mere transience.

Have you ever gotten that inner urge, the impulse to do something in your life, a desire to express yourself—and yet you did not? Have you ever recoiled due to the well-indented yet diverse advice of those close to you who did not agree with you? Have you ever buried anything deep inside to hide from public mockery, so as not to threaten your social existence? I have—more than once. This time, though, it's different. I cannot escape the transformation that is overpowering my coherent will.

This book arose out of a personal quest for truth and the need to finally express myself amid the process of letting go of the darkness inside. It had screamed within, in hope of recognition. Every attempt at denial, a suppressed cover-up, painfully reminded me to take notice. The moment has occurred! I did it! This book is an expression of my soul that has long awaited its revelation. It is my turning point into the unknown, and those who will be drawn to it are the same ones who are in the process of transformation that is reshaping my life too.

Nonetheless, this is not meant to be some absolute truth, but rather a humble witness to my own journey and the knowledge that I have gathered along the road. Its purpose is to learn and grow on a personal level, but perhaps it can also encourage those who are in doubt about which way to go. This is my very personal truth, but still, I'm sure, by some wonder, it will find a connection with the truths of other souls on their journey, in the same way a drop of water finds a spring by the air we all breathe, the ground over which we tread, and the light that we all equally bestow. Seemingly apart, each one on its own, still we are connected like islands in the depths of oceans by land that is invisible to the eye of a nescient observer.

PART ONE

In Search of a Time Lost: The Early Years

"He who has a why to live can bear almost any how."

—*Friedrich Nietzsche*

June 1997

I sat motionless on the terrace, with the smell of salt in my nostrils coming from the seaside, absorbed by the still darkness of a house that had never felt like home. It seemed as if an eternity swept in front of me in a flash and had me trapped, imprisoned by my own pride, filled with guilt and spite, embittered and lost. Within the blink of an eye, memories rushed by of a childhood I did not want to remember and then seemed to have been gone forever, lost in the darkness of my own feelings, in a torrent that threatened to overflow. Here and there, some blurry flashes of a giggle appeared in the memory of my alienated past. An attempt to keep pace with the music emerged as the radio generated some danceable tunes; an occasional moan coming from my dance partner, older sister Maria, and the sight of Mom and Dad, who danced in rhythm with us. Occasionally, some other memories were summoned up, and they seemed to witness the beauty of growing up in a big family but, as by a veil of secrecy, they were hidden and closely guarded in the depths of my very troubled soul. It seemed as if they surfaced now, quite randomly, the unappealing patches of my covert despair and, finally, the question emerged:

Why did it have to happen to me?

Early Childhood in Croatia (1967-1974)

I was the second child out of five that our mother had boldly brought into the world in only eight years. Five aging adults also lived with us in the house, at a time when our very existence depended on the fishing earnings of our father. One could say that we were poor and underprivileged, but growing up in a large family in a small island village in Croatia had its advantages too. Often, the only thing that disturbed the profound peace of this alienated place was the shouting of children or the echoes that rang when mothers, on the verge of evening, summoned their children to come home. The clutter and the noise would soon recede into the arms of an early evening, which greeted the village in the chimes of church bells ringing. Curled up in front of the radio—as if vicinity meant anything—we would eagerly await the bedtime story.

I was fascinated by the mystique of the stories that were told; on occasion, I listened very carefully, trying to absorb every single word. Apart from mandatory schoolbooks, we had no other children's books in the house. The stories we were familiar with were either passed on to us by the elderly, in the same traditional manner the stories had been passed down to them for centuries before, or during evening gatherings around a big, old radio that was our only link to the world outside the isolated island.

I can also remember my father telling us stories while we picked ripe olives from wet grass into baskets in front of us, fingers trembling with cold. He shared stories of Tarzan that were embedded in his mind as a reminiscence of the years he had spent in the army. A picture of my serene grandfather is still clear in my mind, as he used to hoist me into his lap prior to my bedtime and speak heartedly of the nine years he had spent in the Austro-Hungarian army until he finally found his way back home.

Blabbermouth that I was, I enjoyed retelling and making up stories inspired by the enthusiastic claps of approval of those listening to me, satisfying my driving need for attention. The world of stories attracted me and rekindled my imagination, as did the adult world, filled with mysticism—though shrouded by a veil of secrecy that I often, in my immature mind, could not even begin to understand. Too often to count, I would, in my gleeful and spontaneous curiosity, attract the attention of many older people. This was especially true of the widowed women who had requested my company; I would, with consent from my parents, spend many nights with them after the death of their spouses. I don't know why I continually agreed to share their burden, because I was, in fact, afraid of all those places where the recently estranged souls had lived, prior to their departure from this world. I feared the old ladies with their black scarves tied tightly around their necks and their dark, grave attires. At the same time, I was, in some indefinable way, attracted to them by the power that was stronger than my fragile will.

I can still remember the thin silhouette of a once-strong uncle on the eve of his long-anticipated death as I joyfully unraveled a story, one that he had once told me. I remember being unafraid when, in the depths of his eyes, I could observe the serenity that came over him and the tranquility that dominated in knowledge that was beyond my reach. After his death, it almost seemed to have become a ritual that I spent a lot of time with his widow, accompanying her around day and night like a shadow. In the time that followed, I got acquainted with the dark impulses of the same old retinue with whom I had spent many preceding evenings. Some of them, whom I had known very well, and one was another old uncle, did not hesitate to expose me to his dirty little games that I could never figure out: flashing his genitals when no one was looking or reaching to touch mine as I lay squeezed between him and his wife on my sleepover nights. This made me draw back and retreat, to suppress the events that had come to pass. Eventually, ashamed and afraid to tell my parents for fear of condemnation, I gave up socializing with those who had hurt me so unexpectedly. The memories of senseless wounding I then deposited in the deepest layers of my infant soul, trying to prevent them from ever rising to the surface again. I was never the same again. I spent the next summer away from familiar faces, thus carefully avoiding my parents and the gentle company of my sisters, as I watched them in envy of their innocence. Although too young and inexperienced, I gladly accepted the invitation to help my widowed aunt and her only son by working odd jobs around their small boarding house. Small wonder that, in spite of my age, I felt no burden of the working hours while peeling potatoes in the hot morning sun with a blunt knife or while, in the late evenings while barely awake, I washed the last glasses from the tables that were emptied as the guests withdrew to their rooms.

The Promised Land (1974-1984)

Restless in soul but with a new severity, I started school at the ripe age of seven, and I remember it seemed obvious that my folks were more than relieved by the fact that I had finally quieted down, even though they had not realized the extent of my profound changes. I soon found out that good grades in school consequently attracted certain benefits—idle time and status in the family, so I pooled all my efforts into trying to maintain the status, once again regaining the sought-after attention of my parents.

Three years passed peacefully in the illusion of my mediocre existence, and then on one seemingly ordinary day, my father's female cousin mysteriously arrived. Her name was Maria, as was my sister's. Well-groomed and snappy, with beauty like that of a prominent movie star, her blonde hair at shoulder length and a pearly smile on her face, she instilled awe. Her posture expressed pride and status, but in her slightly small and narrowed eyes the truth prevailed. Behind the polite sternness of her pleasing features with which she easily imposed herself upon others, the eyes hid pain and loneliness that had been revealed for a split second, too quick for anyone to notice. She was all wrapped up in a mystery that allured me.

Curiously, but with caution, I circled the kitchen, only to brush up at the table where my parents silently whispered in her company, all the while not forgetting to express my polished yet slightly forced manners. "Good day! . . . Enjoy! . . . How are you?" and so on. I couldn't even imagine that just those few short sentences would lead to my first long trip away from home. A year later, at the age of ten, accompanied by the still-mysterious cousin Maria—or Aunt Maria, as I had preferred to call her later—with my parents' silent but slightly unsecure blessing and a handful of farewell advice of the mostly aged villagers, I left everything I knew behind and made my way to America.

The journey proved to be a real adventure, but problems arose from the very start at our destination. In those first days of my venture, I felt a grim wave of change that had me overtaken. Despite my overwhelming curiosity, exhilaration, and considerable resourcefulness, I had to admit that I did not like the situation I obviously had to face. Vast and seemingly inhospitable, the smog-polluted city that had replaced the simplicity of my recent habitat had not been as inviting as I had anticipated. I was sickened by the boiling heat of the asphalt that had caused me to back out at times, in fear of entering the gas-polluted car. I yearned for the green expanses of my far-off home, in remembrance of my bare feet on cool grass and rocks immersed in the warmth of the summer sea.

It those first few awkward days, we visited more shopping malls than I could ever have dreamed of existing, buying more things than I had ever before possessed in my short life. In addition, I occupied a room in our apartment far too spacious for my petty needs, with a huge walk-in closet and a bathroom of my own, a pure luxury. Despite my apparent admiration of the vast lodgings, and due to my aunt's evident effort to make me feel at home, I could not block out the memory of my older sister, Maria. It was she with whom I had previously shared a single bed each night, each on one end of the bed, in a room where our grandparents slept too, our restless legs jostling for space.

All curled up and alone in the vastness of the great fairy-tale bedroom, I could hardly resist the nightmares that had plagued me with the first hint of a dream. Even now, I can still see the contours of that which had troubled me in those first nights—a witch who had me restrained and a bulky snake that had repeatedly appeared in my dreams in an attempt to prevent me from crossing the road. In the sleepless agony of morbid and terrifying fear, I would wake up and stare at the darkness, hopelessly fighting sleep, only until the same repeated again and again. After a few nights of pure horror, I had finally gathered the courage to crawl into my aunt's bed, shyly touching her feet for support. Just then, a tingling feeling arose from the heart, creating a craving for the warmth of my older sister, whom I had so immeasurably missed.

In those early summer months, on work days, while my aunt worked in a West Covina pediatric clinic, I would patiently spend my days in a summer camp and, too often, I would prompt myself an hour or so earlier to sit on a bench in front of the high fence, awaiting the moment when she would appear on the other side. Though comfortless and silent in a quiet despair that would overcome, on those rare occasions Aunt Maria seemed to be the only present glimmer of light, and I was honestly delighted when I caught sight of her. From our earliest beginnings, the two of us had never exchanged much more than a mere gentle word or a frown, and the air was always filled with an ambiguity that had sealed off all attempts at a warm and cozy relationship right from the start.

I do not remember a lot of socializing with other children in those early days, and I knew I was gently being bypassed by most of them because of a mutual inability to communicate properly. I studied English along the way, with the help of a tutor twice a week during summer, but it was mostly due to Aunt Maria and her relentless questioning that I had learned many new words on a daily basis. It was obvious that academic achievement was important to her, so I invested extra time and effort, in order to earn her praise. I had also loosened up enough in summer school to enter a competition that earned me a respectable blue ribbon for my artwork. I was thrilled because I had miraculously surpassed even my own expectations. Somehow, the achievement made me feel connected to my father who, on rare occasions, as he drew out an old sketchbook from his wooden chest, had thus demonstrated his own enviable art skills. With new determination, I decided to devote some time to developing these skills, and Aunt Maria, noticing the fresh glimmer, had supported my pursuit.

In the fall, even though there was still much to be learned regarding my English, I was quite ready for school. With better knowledge of the language, it was easier to fit into the school's small society. Right from the start, my attention was drawn to a girl named Pamela, whom, I had later learned, was the only survivor of a tragedy that struck her family, in which her parents and a younger sister had been killed in a car crash. On the first day of school, while I had timidly leaned against the school wall, she came to ask me, "Do you miss your mom and dad?" The question hit my heart, and it seemed to draw air from my lungs as intense feelings took charge. I could not answer, for it had awakened an avalanche that I had carefully hidden away.

In time, though, fascinated by the new opportunities at hand, the acquired knowledge of the English language, and by the hint of a first true friendship, I had quickly learned to hide yet again the feelings for my distant home. But despite the brilliant new friends and acquaintances, my heart had, in that short period of time, absorbed enough emptiness and yearning to last a lifetime. I wrote letters almost every day, at the beginning with a little help of Aunt Maria, who taught me all the formalities of writing a decent letter. I wrote many letters to my sister Maria in particular, whom I had, surprisingly enough, missed more than I missed my parents. Letters, it seemed, were my only contact with the reality that I had left behind. A deep desire and longing soon turned into unbearable pain as I waited for the postman's truck with a letter from home.

The year passed, and with a California summer emerging, we left it all to visit my family in Croatia. Words cannot describe the joy I felt then, even stricken by the knowledge that it was only temporary. In the few short summer weeks, I tried to catch up on *everything* that I had missed out on during the year abroad, but the differences that had already occurred were more than obvious. One quick look at myself in my flattering, colorful dresses—compared with the worn-out garments of my sisters—said enough in favor of the differences that had been imposed upon us. The desire to be more like my sisters had driven me to act unadvisedly, as I handed each one a dress of my own and kept the last for myself. When I returned to America, I experienced a revelation in the shock of learning that I had not been allowed to do so. Forced to write a letter to my mother to ask for the return of my dresses, I felt the reluctance and spite that were not there before. The package with the dresses arrived soon enough, but in my unspoken protest during the rest of the year, I wore a single dress, the one with which I had returned.

My heart was absorbed by gaps of awkward silence that accompanied the whole event, only to deepen the abysses of our relationship and my despair. I was miserable in the knowledge that I no longer shared things with my sisters, and the abundance of my own possessions did nothing to mend a broken heart. At night, hidden by the darkness of my room, I wept silent tears of sorrow. I built new walls to defend myself from hurt, putting chains around my heart in order to protect the feelings of sadness that came to overflow. In the years that followed, as if in silent agreement, Aunt Maria and I did not mention the inconvenience of our beginnings. There were some pleasant moments I can recall, too—the refreshing weekend walks along the beach and relaxed conversations of the heart—but they only marked a deep, committed tie of two wounded souls and the attempts that had remained just that. Of different age, varying on the outside but similar within, seeking affection that was neither given nor received, my aunt and I were careful not to intervene with the bitter existence of our common deficiencies.

Just before my thirteenth birthday, we flew back for another short visit at home. It was May, with school still in session, and it all somehow gave a deeper mark to what happened the following day. Confined to a small, stuffy office of the Social Service Center in Zadar, my parents, Aunt Maria, and I took turns talking to a psychiatrist. It made no sense at first, but by the end of the morning, I was finally briefed about the official adoption that had taken place there and then, and I remember how I could not understand the significance, but I played along. Some time had passed between that moment and the next, when I painfully learned that, in fact, the adoption was to seal my fate further.

Years passed in our silent agreement to manage the situation at hand. I shifted my focus to school achievements, along with an occasional devotion to the painting easel and a clumsy flick through my guitar strings. There was no significant time spent hanging out with peers because my life was overly crowded by the elderly once again—Aunt Maria as she was getting ready to retire, her stern and dominant mother, and an easygoing uncle of hers in his nineties whose health was deteriorating quickly.

With his wife ill in a nursing home and having no children, he had, upon my aunt's invitation, agreed to live with us. We were surely an unusual bunch, gathered together in a very peculiar way, each in hiding from his or her true feelings.

Beyond a doubt, to an uninformed observer, my life could have easily seemed like an interesting adventure or even the fulfillment of a poor child's dream. Unlike my brother and sisters, I lived in abundance, lacking nothing, or so it seemed. Aunt Maria was a respected pediatrician with more than a decent income who had, only by her own iron will and determination, slowly worked her way up the social ladder, proving herself worthy of respect in the States and back home. She had come to know poverty and the shortcomings of it well throughout her own life, so she openly praised the privileges of the upper class and didn't hide her disappointment when I failed to recognize and respect its benefits too. Perhaps, engulfed by her own grief, she was unable to notice that my heart was filled with a gap that no object could ever fulfill. I longed for the only form of fulfillment I had not been offered: the proximity to my immediate family and the company of peers.

Once again, I started to dream about returning home, but right then the implication, which had been caused by my adoption, began to re-appear. Things had indeed changed drastically, and sometimes I seriously considered taking the opportunity to escape from everything by running away. But my rational mind was too quick to assure me of the possible failure of such a venture. After a while, during my sophomore year of high school, I had decided to challenge my aunt with a proposal which, to my astonishment, she had accepted, clearly underestimating the power of the burning desire within me. She uttered fatally, "Okay, you can spend the next school year in Croatia, but if you fail to finish the year with honors, you will come back." It was agreed with glory on my part.

She was convinced that I would fail, but I knew otherwise. And so, once again, my life took an abrupt turn, and I began to make arrangements for my return.

Back in the Old Country (1984-1986)

My excitement quickly withered. Even though I did return to Croatia, I never actually returned *home*. When school started, Aunt Maria, still taking care of her uncle, returned to Los Angeles, and I was left to live with her peevish mother, whose health was rapidly worsening, along with her years-long faithful but disillusioned maid in a villa by the sea of an exclusive part of Zadar. As months passed, it seemed as if my freedom was even more eroded by school errands and the leash that I was on. My social life took another fall into the space between departures and returns from school. Lonelier than ever, I had estranged myself to the premises of my room, occupied with assignments, so as to avoid confronting the obvious.

Aunt Maria, for what it's worth, did not make my challenge any easier, and when she left for the States, I had already started to attend a very prominent high school class. This lifted the criteria even more, as we went on to take the title as best in our generation in Zadar. The nineteen new subjects that I had to deal with were way too much, more than I had even anticipated, and on top of that, to make up for my freshman and sophomore year abroad, eleven more emerged. It wasn't just a matter of studying hard; it was a matter of excelling in each area if I ever meant to accomplish the goal that I had set for myself—staying in Croatia permanently.

Without much useless analysis, I found myself dealing with the problem at hand, most of the time keeping to myself, confined to my room, studying even when I thought I couldn't anymore. At the end of my junior year, I sought my prize—I had finished the year with honors. It was a stunt that no one had expected, least of all my aunt Maria. When the time came, she was forced by her word given to accept defeat. Albeit reluctantly, she blessed my further stay in Croatia. Little did I know at the time that there was nothing to rejoice about! I had nothing to show for my efforts. I was still separated from my family, and the few encounters with them did not significantly ease my loneliness. I sensed then that something was horribly wrong, and as time elapsed, I found myself totally estranged from those I had once called my family. Nothing was ever the same again.

For the first time, I seriously began to doubt and mistrust my parents. There was a sour feeling of being estranged that started to arise within, while my whole world just seemed to have collapsed before my eyes. There was a gap afloat that had piled up over the years, and it happened in me and in those with whom I met again, seemingly insurmountable. The futile attempt to return to some familiar reality was no longer a possibility. I thought, *Oh, God, they have all changed,* but the truth was that *I* had changed, and I was not the same person anymore. On one particular evening, in the surge of despair, I had even tried to escape, but I soon realized that those to whom I confided only acted to stop me. Lost in faith, I started to feel the rebel in me rising to the surface.

At the beginning of my senior year, my aunt's mother died, but I was the one feeling like the ghost of the house. Confined to myself, I had clearly lost all hope of ever finding my home again. Aunt Maria arrived for the funeral and remained for a short time thereafter. I was naive enough to believe that somehow things might change. In a desperate attempt to explain my feelings to my parents and my aunt, I had only worsened the already murky conditions of my life. When my father arrived to talk with Aunt Maria, I noticed instantly that dejected, humble, and quiet manner of his, and I knew I stood no chance, but I still decided to give it a try. I understood his burden, as it had, for a long time, been a valid reason for me too, to stay back and obey in an effort to please. My aunt had, in fact, a few years earlier, saved my father's life at a time when he was diagnosed with kidney cancer and was literally sent home from the hospital to die.

I remember well the day when Dad came home from the hospital, because it was midsummer, and I was about to leave for Los Angeles. I remember how my father handed some papers over to me with trembling hands and how he made me promise that I would show them to Aunt Maria. I remember my aunt's face as I handed the papers over to her. She dialed a number and angrily shouted into the receiver. I remember it well, even though I was only twelve years old, because it was the day before Mom came down the stairs in the morning, her body crouched with signs of panic. She walked inconsolably, and her auburn hair was newly covered with silvery-whitish spots of gray. When Aunt Maria ended the unpleasant conversation of the first call, she then dialed a second number and, in a milder tone, arranged an urgent transfer for my father to another hospital in Croatia. The surgery within the next two days had ultimately saved his life, and he is alive and well to this day because of it.

I can imagine how stricken my father might have felt back then, as I stood so adamant to get my life back. I did not stop, even after he had begged me to. The words just slid from my lips, painfully accusing the ones present, and at least for that brief moment, I felt some of the burden disappear. But it was just a flicker in a moment, and in the minutes that were followed by the silent respect of the adults in front of me, I knew I had lost the battle and the war as well. The last spark of joy and hope faded before me.

The episode ended abruptly with my sudden relocation to the home of my father's older sister, who stared at me with suspicion, reluctantly providing temporary accommodation so that I could finish high school. If I had ever wanted to die, it was then. I remember the whispers of those who thought they knew me, the directed fingers, the mocking, and the ridicule and malicious objections of those who did not know my grief but went out of their way to undermine the little dignity that was left in me. On rare occasions, in the expectation of support, I would go to the island to visit my parents, my head bent, ashamed, miserable, and gloomy, in anticipation of compassion that had been lost somewhere. My heart bled with grief as I sensed betrayal, but I hid the conceived wounds behind seamlessly disguised defiance. It had started to form within awhile back and came to present itself toward anyone who tried to make a pass at me. Back at school, thanks to the perseverance and support of my unusual friend Tamara, despite the fear, humiliation, and obvious social discrepancies, it all ended with praise.

Within the premises of Zadar Music School, in the presence of a few selected, with a special program to honor the best students of the generation, lonely and dull, I sat alone. Meanwhile, the school principal went on to inform the audience about my unusual academic achievements, never suspecting that those challenges to me were nothing compared to what lay ahead. I was like a wounded beast, aching and sensitive. I growled for time lost, and with each new day, I pulled away further from my family and my own self. I learned to hide all feelings behind a smile; only a careful observer would notice the hidden message contained in the depths beyond the seemingly joyful sight.

The Escape (1986-1996)

It was obvious that my leaving Aunt Maria had disappointed my family, just as it was obvious that many gloated over it. Some family members passed on their judgments as they openly convicted my actions, and it seemed that besides my best friend, Tamara, and my sister Maria, I could not find a trace of genuine compassion or support anywhere. The revolt that steadily enhanced within was wrapped up and suppressed in grief mixed with the overwhelming feeling that I had ultimately disappointed myself. With nowhere to turn except to my own still-distinguished desire to succeed, I went on to get a degree in education but was forced to stay within affordable premises in the city of Zadar.

At the age of twenty-one, I found myself in the same small village that I had left as a ten-year-old, now married to an equally lost and wounded but fragile soul. By that time, I had landed a job in a nearby elementary school. At the same time, my first son, Frane, was born. He was big and strong, yet calm and quiet, a bit introverted, serious and mysterious in his own ways. Even though he might have come unexpectedly and much too soon for me to adapt, I was filled with quiet pride and joy as I watched him grow. I worked in the school for most of the next ten years. The lovely children I had encountered there became a good cause to fight for while trying to forget my own misfortunes. I will never forget their smiling faces. In those uncertain years, which had been marked by a civil war in Croatia and time spent with my son, Frane, the ten frail years of my marriage quickly swept by with clarity that was evident; we had become mere strangers to each other. The two of us were like two distant islands, apparently totally different but essentially related in depths of our souls by indisputable suffering that had destroyed our lives on a daily basis. I retained my shaky balance, jostling between Frane and my work at school. My ex-husband chose to drown his sorrows in alcohol.

Lost, angry, embarrassed, and alone without the support and compassion of my immediate family, once again I felt abandoned and lonesome—even more so as I turned thirty and found out that I was pregnant for the second time. Through my veins, instead of blood, sadness and misery flowed in streams and threatened to occupy every cell of my body. But then, at the time of my greatest distress, what happened then changed the outcome of my wish for death.

In the moments of my withdrawal, in the absence of consolation, I confided to high concrete walls I had built around myself. I was not ready for the event that followed.

The Moment of Clarity (June 1997)

It seemed like the beginning of a very ordinary day. A gloomy morning, hidden under swollen clouds, contributed to the severity of the atmosphere in the classroom. The work brought departure from the reality that befell me. In the midst of a quiet moment, while the children's heads were leaning over an assignment in front of them, I had found myself at an abnormally high standpoint, staring at my own bent head over a desk in the middle of the classroom. For the flicker of a moment, it seemed, I viewed the scene, and then I was back in my body, while the morbid silence endured awhile longer. I raised my head, only to see little heads bowed and busy in a task. My heart began to pound harder, and the blood gushed in streams into my brain as I tried to recall, *Is it morning or afternoon?* A nervous glance out the window did not reveal the secret. *What are the children doing?* A short walk through the aisles informed me that the children were engaged in a language assignment. *What time is it?* I looked at my digital watch, but it betrayed me with no signs of life. In disbelief, I took it off my wrist and left it on the table. At an accelerated pace, I rushed to open the door into the hallway and glanced at the clock. It pointed in silence and showed 10:20 a.m. "It's morning," I whispered to myself and remembered that the bell should ring in five minutes to summon the children to recess. I was relieved.

Pacing up, recalling within the next few minutes the event that had come to pass, I remembered that it was a Tuesday. Still in shock, I told the few colleagues present in the staff room of the unusual event. In the silence that followed, I could discern the alluded compassion and concern, which only added to my even greater confusion. I soon regretted that I shared such an intimate event with the attendees. A voice echoed through my head louder than some others, *How cool! You have power!* I was reeling in my head, and it seemed sickening. I do not remember how I managed to endure through the end of the workday, but when I got home, I felt chills when I sat in silence, working up a plan for yet another departure. The school year was almost over. I welcomed the end of the summer with two suitcases and a bag in each hand, with the ten-year-old Frane and a six-month-old pregnancy. We moved away to the nearest city, wishing for a fresh, new start.

Since then, in the years that followed, with many ties cut off from my previous life and due to the loneliness and despair, the many rented flats, the struggle to take care of my children, and the sacred intent to make a decent living, I have learned the most.

To Fear, Suffer, and Sacrifice

"Life is simple, it's just not easy."

—Author unknown

It seemed as if fear and suffering had been my faithful companions for many years that had marked my childhood, adolescence, and a greater part of my adulthood, until the moment I realized that I needed to let go of it once and for all. The recognition of the power to change that which has been so deeply ingrained within was as scary as it was liberating. It was also time-consuming. Sometimes it seemed to have been an impossible mission, in search of a way out of the world of misguided understanding, to find the right path, time, and strength for the reversal. In moments of my withdrawal, the query thoughts of the purpose of suffering appeared, which I did not pretend to understand. Those were the times when I had to admit to myself that I feared fear itself and that I was simply afraid of letting it go. I did not know how to get rid of fear, how to abandon anger and rage, when it seemed as if those were the only things that had made me real most of my life. I had hung on to them as if they were a life vest, but instead they made me even more helpless.

Rooted in the only reality that I knew, cocooned, lonely, full of mistrust, and hurt but adamant to make a change that would count, I decided to take a look at my life from another perspective. I chose to give forgiveness a chance.

The mere decision of forgiveness was not as difficult as the process itself, which proved to be a resolution that would take a long time to resolve. Nonetheless, my intention was pure and clear. I decided to change the circumstances of my life, and it was clear to me that I needed to start embracing even the most hardened parts of my wounded soul. In moments of solitude, when the night surrounded me with peace and quiet, I struggled with the depths of darkness inside of me.

Eventually, I brought to light the ghosts of my past and wrote down their names on a piece of paper. And when the time arrived, when I was ready to face them, staring into the depths within each one, these ghosts, so consciously awakened on paper, were mostly names of the ones that I had cherished the most. I was reluctant to forgive and afraid to forget, but I knew that I had to go through with it—to let go of the feeling of having been sacrificed, a feeling that had so faithfully accompanied me every step of the way for more than thirty years of my life.

The realization that I would eventually have to claim responsibility for my life came next. Crammed with new fear, desperate yet determined, in the solitude of night, I shed tears; they came out in streams that had been hidden somewhere deep inside of me, and they came flooding, unstoppably powerful. For years, sadness, despair, and anger accumulated and piled up in thick layers around my heart, and the uncoiling lasted longer than my expectations had. Just when I thought that they were out of sight, I would find new clutter that I would devotedly deal with again and again. If forgiveness was not such a big thing, the letting go surely seemed impossible sometimes. It meant accepting—to consciously release that which I did not understand, accept that everything had happened in a way that was filled with greater purpose, and that it had an ultimate goal—that of my own healing.

It was annoying to find out that even straight As, which I had easily acquired in school, were not a guarantee of later success and did nothing to ensure the knowledge of the most important topics in life. The unstoppable desire to discover the essence of life, the purpose of existence, the hope to reveal the reasons that hid behind what I had experienced as personal sacrifice suddenly began to take over. Suffering regained its true meaning only when I realized that it was perhaps the most important lesson that I had not yet learned. When I did not recognize its meaning, because it was hidden behind piles of pain and hurt, destiny tossed an even more difficult task my way, yet another wound accompanied with pain. And when I did not recognize the purpose again, suffering only increased. Had I not embraced and confronted it at last, I am sure that it would have taken me, almost certainly, to a premature death.

To forgive is to forget, to leave the past in the past. This was a lesson hard learned. Even what may seem easy for others somehow proved to be most difficult for me—to forgive myself. I justified my own self-criticism by criticizing others. I believed that I had the right to expect excellence from everyone because I expected even more from myself. On the contrary, though, the higher my expectations were, the bigger the disappointments too. I ran this vicious cycle for a very long time. Today, looking back, I often wonder:

What would have happened if I had not come to understand that it is all up to me?

How long would I have suffered, and how long would I have destroyed myself and others as well?

Is it possible that letting go results in healing?

Can we learn without suffering?

Is suffering really necessary?

I strongly believe that suffering, though basically neither good nor bad, is not really necessary. But in some ways, it is our own choice, a lesson adapted to a person's style of learning. My suffering was uniquely mine. I would hardly agree with the saying I've heard repeatedly: "Smart people learn from other people's mistakes." How many times I've heard that sentence, and yet I believe that the lessons of one's own experience are the only ones that really prompt change on a personal level. And while we may empathize with others, we cannot say that other people's misery can affect us as our own. It is certainly easier to forget pain that is not ours. We are witnesses to that every day. As for learning from other people's mistakes, I can confidently say that, despite constant reminders, I had not.

We are all pupils of the path of life. Every moment of existence is always new and knowledge-providing. Still, "Happiness does not teach anything," my wise teacher, Boris, used to say. I did not understand that at the time, but I learned it to be true, from personal experience. Happiness and misfortune, along with all other opposite states of this world, exist for a purpose. We cannot enjoy happiness if we have never been troubled, just as a person born blind will never be able to experience light, no matter how strong the desire. We learn from our own experience. The experience of suffering forces us to examine the deepest abysses of ourselves, and it may seem dark and time-consuming, useless and unnecessary to undergo such hardship, but it awakens the soul and it brings us closer to who we really are.

Acceptance or Denial

With each new day, we broaden our experience. We choose either acceptance or denial. Each time we choose denial, we choose to forget to notice; we ignore the message from life itself. Acceptance enables the flow. It is a sweet surrender of the will, a fulfilling sacrifice, and a release that pleases the heart. Of course, life is not always simple. It is not easy to understand or accept. A child's death or the suffering of a mass of people—how can one justify it? Nevertheless, we always have a choice—to accept or not to accept; to act or not to act. And always, there are consequences to deal with. Everything we choose teaches us a lesson. When we are ready to accept a lesson that life offers, we can move on to the next lesson. The essence of life is learning, growth, development, personal improvement, and ultimately the collective, the evolution of mankind.

I believe that the biggest challenge of acceptance is surrender, the decision to sacrifice the old beliefs for something new, which implies that it is for the highest good.

Can we accept the sacrifice of our old beliefs for a higher good?

Can we have faith long enough to perceive the outcome?

It is all up to us. We can continue to do as we have always done, or we can embrace change. We can let go of old thoughts and feelings. To let go means to get rid of excess weight on our shoulders, to tune up and coordinate ourselves with the pleasant, effortless, graceful fluid of life. This fine sensibility develops over years of learning, and we should not be discouraged if we find it to be difficult. Accepting that which we need to let go carries the seed of growth and prosperity within it. It is the dawning of a different life, and it is so relieving that we will never want to go back to where we were before. To let go of the troubled past is to make a giant leap into one's own fulfillment. It is just incredible how things start to change on the outside when you find the courage to change within. It has never been about changing others. It has always been about changing that which troubles you most within yourself, "being the change that you want to see in others."

For years, I've tried to forgive my parents, and now I am sure I have succeeded, because the reflection is so obvious. I can feel their remission, the relief and ease of going that has not been there before. *It has happened only because of what I chose to do on my own.* I've learned that the best way to change others is to accept them and change oneself within. Somehow, then the change will manifest on the outside too. Accepting those who have hurt me in the past was an annoying mission for quite a long time, and the mere thought that I would have to accept and change *myself* and not *them* sometimes seemed awkward and absurd. It was hard to accept. But the power lies within acceptance. Everything around us is a mirror image of our thoughts and feelings. The only way to change what we do not like is by turning to ourselves. We have the power of change, but it obligates us to change ourselves first, to take responsibility, to grow, and to learn.

We all grow at our own pace; hence the differences in opinion among us. We should not compare ourselves to others, because it entails forgetting who we are. We are not like anyone else. No one should have to be a copy of anyone else.

Suffering inflicts pain because we are afraid. It haunts us because we try to escape from it. To be strong and not waver, to be brave and not afraid, to love suffering rather than trying to flee from it is to taste its deep, sweet surrender. The resistance is what hurts. Suffering is a just a personal conception of the mind. It's as real as you make it out to be.

But is sacrifice really necessary?

Can it be justified with some past or future moment?

I met an older gentleman once who told me his life story. He had founded his company in his early twenties and worked long hours in his garage, dreaming and building a stable life for his family. He worked hard, and the business grew. The more it flourished, the more time he invested in maintaining and organizing the business. The more he built, the less time he had for himself and his family. He continued to work hard, ignoring signs of health problems. He was busy and devoted, and slowly he had built a business empire. He did not even stop then. The more he acquired, the more there seemed to still be acquired. One achievement followed another, and he set new goals each time. He galloped relentlessly, not stopping until he was chained to a hospital bed, his heart painfully reminding him to examine his life. In the moment when his whole life flashed before his eyes, he rendered a decision. He went on to sell his company, bought a boat, and settled down. Nowadays, you might spot him, his sails outstretched, as he sails the Adriatic Sea for half of the year in the company of his wife. He spends the rest of the year with his family and friends.

Can we learn from his story? Of course we can, but we will not. Because we all have our own unique life challenges to meet.

Shall we therefore cease to wish, dream, or work? Will we replace the material exclusively with the spiritual and live as ascetics? Of course not, unless it is our path to follow; but whatever we do, it will always be exclusively our choice, the path we have chosen to stride, one that no one else has walked before—the truly unknown. As much as we constantly listen about the trodden and the less-trodden paths, and how the brave always choose the less-trodden ones, I can confidently say that my journey has always been just mine, and the only person who had walked it has been me. Bravery has nothing to do with it—it's just a fact of life, a step we must dare take. We all walk the unknown every day. There are those who accompany us for a while; some follow, and sometimes we follow others. We meet some along the way, share a sequence maybe, or only meet at the crossroads—we always walk a unique path. It's one and only, each for itself. Many times, though, we pace to take control of the path ahead of us, but I wonder:

Does the rigid, controlled way of life preclude us from the magic?

Do we try to fulfill and satisfy aspirations that are not ours?

Will we ever fully live this sacred existence if we don't stop and ask ourselves—which way is *my* own way?

Can we loosen enough to be part of the flow without the will to control?

Can we have faith in the letting go of controls, which enables us to encounter even greater achievements?

We may not find the answers to all these questions at once, but we will die trying. Our physical body will surely die, sooner or later. How will we live? What will we learn? It will all depend upon the decisions that we make every day: whether we choose left or right, forward or backward, acceptance or denial, to live in the now, in faith, or within the fiction of our minds.

Life is choice, and everything in it is a choice. The knowledge that there is no wrong way is hidden in the freedom of variety, but only one way that we ourselves have chosen is our unique way, and it is interwoven with a network of roads of other people we encounter in life.

What is the meaning of life?

To live is to accept that we are unique in this world, that our path is just ours and as such is not subject to any comparisons. We face challenges every day: Which path to choose? Where to start? Where to turn? Most of the time, the choices we make—whether we are aware of it or not—arise out of a desire to please others or out of fear of what others might think or say about us. Freedom of choice means being able to choose what feels right, even though it may not agree with the reason of our own intellect or the intellect of others.

Many of us do not do what feels right, what makes us happy, but rather that which is expected. Afraid to follow the heart, we soon come to realize that we are not satisfied with our lives.

We become angry and defensive and deny that the choices were ours to make. Setting goals, careful planning and execution of the predetermined confirm every day that we operate to keep the strings in our hands. "Take control of your life!" What does that even mean? The control itself is a worthless play of the mind if your well-being is in the future tense. The future may never present itself, since we can only live in the now.

Rapture is just a moment in existence, but joyfulness can be a state.

Driven by the need to control, we plan and strive toward a single moment in life when, in fact, we can stop to feel the joy in the totality of existence. We often choose not to stop until we achieve our goals, even if the goal is not ours to pursue.

Can we stop to notice a single moment?

Can we accept it?

We can even accept that something is unacceptable. There is no wrong or right. There are no two of the same paths, just as there are no two of the same people. The essence of freedom is recognizing our own. Even when there is no external freedom, even if we are chained, we can choose to either accept or not accept. It is our right and our choice either way.

> *"The process of change does not occur on superficial levels, through mere 'positive thinking.' It involves exploring, discovering, and changing our deepest, most basic attitudes toward life."*
>
> **—Shakti Gawain**

The Past, Present, and Future

*"Whenever you overcome compulsive thinking,
then you avoid the reality.*

You do not want to be where you are. Here and Now."

—Eckhart Tolle

When I was a small child, life was all about being able to
play. I lived for the moment, for the game, and the only thing
that was subject to planning was time for homework. That
would allow me, as soon as possible, to rush out of the house
to play soccer with boys. I did not play with dolls, partly
because I didn't have any, and mostly because the thrill of
the action was what captured my interest. I had often left
behind my physically gentler sisters in a different game,
only to follow my own accelerated, more "male" energy. My
obsession was movement, and not to my mother's delight. I
was the first one to wake up and the last to fall asleep each
day. When I was four, I discovered the magic of water and
the salty sea; I swam and jumped with much older children,
diving into the depths until I was out of air. I paddled the

canoe until my arms hurt. I lived for the moment, in the now, and until recently, I had never given it much thought. It was a time taken for granted.

Life in L.A. definitely shifted my perspective from *now* into *tomorrow.* From the slow reality of a small village that was caught in a moment in time, I had flown the ocean, but not just that. It seemed as if I had jumped into another time, one that was a thousand times more accelerated. There was nothing coincidental about it. Everything had to be planned. A strict routine, discipline, and focus on some future result soon became an indispensible part of my everyday life. Still, I adapted to it like fish in the sea.

I do not know what had happened that made me get stuck in the past. Was it the first hint of painful longing, a time of recalling the carefree breeze, the smell of salt in the nostrils, or just the time when I was miles away from home, feeling lonely and alienated, missing Mom and Dad and the loud children's game without limits? In any case, the memories began flooding in unstoppably. I was filled with a deep longing and pain; the only thing that had the scent of satisfaction was the idea to go back home. All effort was invested in keeping my vision alive until the time I had finally returned "home." And then fate took quite an unexpected turn, and it seemed as if only space had changed, but time remained the same.

I was stuck.

"Is now today?"

—Antonio, five years old

Have you ever found yourself stuck—whether you were longing for past events, people, or things, or focused on a moment in the future—and you had clearly forgotten to live in the now?

In one way or another, the feeling is surreal. If being aware of oneself in the present moment means being real, then everything else is a fixation in time.

It was only recently that I found out what living in the moment of now meant.

Walking to school, as part of our newly acquired daily routine and as a result of being laid off work after twenty years of experience, I had asked my seven-year-old daughter Sara, "How do you know when something is real, that is it not a dream?"

"When you use your senses and when you feel," she answered instantly, without giving it much thought, and then added, "Mom, you always ask tough questions."

I smiled at her knowingly because we both shared an equal passion for "tough" questions, and she smiled back in response.

I've worked with children for most of my life and have come to trust their practical wit.

I thought about what she had said, and underneath the obvious, some deeper meaning emerged:

> *"Live with full lungs, but stop and listen to the whispering of the wind, hear the birds chirping at dawn, smell the flowers on the hillside, experience*

the taste of a sweet-sour apple in your mouth, enjoy
the beauty of the sunset, touch a panicle of grass, and
feel the pure joy of being."

Whether or not you believe that you are here on Earth just this one time or you believe in reincarnation, it is worthwhile to notice the wonders of creation, motion, appearance, and disappearance, the moment that is given to us, and the one that is to emerge, and to be different from any other so far. It is worthwhile to notice the amazing ease with which everything in nature is created before our eyes, without any effort, very simply just *is*. It is important to remember that we are part of the mystical and unfathomed beauty, a not-so-obvious part of reality where everything is created with ease, down to the tiniest detail: our looks, the color of our eyes, our height, and even the freckles on our face.

Yet, how often do we stop to enjoy this moment?

How often do we get stuck in past events, in our feelings and thoughts?

What is real?

Is it possible that we dream while awake, or have we awakened at all?

Too many times to count, we forget to live. We forget to play.

"If I were a magician and could do something nice
for someone, I would give Mom and Dad a ball to
play with."

—Ana (five years old)

Focusing on what has happened or what will be deprives us of what we can experience now. It deprives us of the magic of being.

> *"Life is what happens to you while you're busy making other plans."*
>
> **—John Lennon**

The Burden of Parenthood

"Smart people allow their children to make mistakes sometimes."

—Mahatma Gandhi

Just recently, as I indulged myself into a talk with my twenty-four year old Frane about ideas that had preoccupied my mind for a long time—living in the moment, in the here and now—I realized the truth: in real life, I often hesitated.

"Don't just talk—live by example," he said simply but boldly. It was a statement, not an accusation, yet it struck me strongly. He was supportive of my willingness to change, and the realization of it had its impact.

All children, not just mine, no matter how old they are, always amaze and inspire me. I see my role as a parent a bit differently now than I did back when I was a child, watching my parents fight their own uncertainties.

As a child, I saw my parents through rose-colored glasses. They were irreplaceable, truthful, and full of love, and that's the picture I carried along to America. The more difficult the situation became, as the tenacity of the relationship with Aunt Maria picked up, the holier became the memories of my parents. The pinkish image slowly faded away in the years that followed and eventually disappeared, only to be transformed again.

What happened?

In the light of the events that had piled up during the years that I was away from home, I had at one time completely lost confidence in my parents and my adoptive mother. For years to come, I had critically analyzed their actions in the vain hope of some kind of change that would satisfy me. I was not comforted by the knowledge that they had difficulties when they were growing up and role models who may not have been role models. I longed for their warmth and understanding. Most of the time, I felt like a victim. The feeling that "nobody understands me" was overwhelming. The more I fought for their attention, the farther away they seemed.

It was only when I found myself enwrapped in the role of being a parent that I came to realize how complex parenthood actually is. One does not attend school to learn about parenting. There are no qualifications to aspire to, and yet it is a role in life that frightens even the brave and ambitious. Even though you need not be perfect, and many variations seem apprehensive at times, society—with its imposed expectations—doesn't allow mistakes to be made. There are expectations that befit the body, the mind, the emotions, and the requirements of society, mostly it seems.

Our children, on the other hand, do not expect us to be perfect, but they do expect and deserve love, honesty, and guidance. Honesty, it seems to me, is often the toughest issue to cradle.

But how can we expect them to deal with their problems if we hide our own?

As I see it, when you eliminate the burden of perfectionism, parenting is not really such a bugaboo. But it takes time and many initial mistakes to realize that.

Today, I remind myself to give my children unconditional love and support on a daily basis, and I learn everything else along the way. I do not fear or feel ashamed to say that I do not know how to solve some situations. To be honest, I have learned some of the toughest lessons by watching my children grow. Nature sometimes plants a reversed role upon us. It is a fact that we all learn from each other, and in life, the most important lessons to learn come in a package called *family*—functional or dysfunctional, it makes us learn and grow.

I admit, I am still not always sure how to proceed in each situation, despite the fact that I am a teacher by profession and have read quite a few books on the topic. The realization that parenthood does not automatically contain the knowhow might even be liberating. Part of the excitement of being a parent is in the magic of not knowing everything—the expectations, the inability to predict every little situation, the touch of everlasting confrontation with the unknown, and ultimately the confrontation with oneself. I am certain that many wonderful things happen that we are unable to even imagine, let alone predict. It is certain that parents do their best, given the level of consciousness at the time. In light of that discovery, the shabby vision of my parents came to life. I began to realize that they too were children once and that they might have had parents just as imperfect as I find myself to be, but they still did the best they knew how. Knowing that I need not be a victim of my parents' misdoings freed me. At some time in life, when we ourselves feel that leap onto a new level of awareness, the things that have troubled us most unwrap speedily. If we are able to see beyond the obvious and start to reclaim responsibility, the changes happen quickly. Once again, we start by forgiving ourselves and those around us and by letting go of old thoughts and habits.

The thing that overwhelmed me was the fact that I had to get rid of the anger that had me swallowed for many long years in the past. It was not a matter of who's right or wrong—it was just a matter of my own conception and the need to see beyond that. The very idea of forgiveness had struck me amid the process of getting rid of old, accumulated burdens that made me stumble every step of the way. My personal quest for meaning and truth had turned my attention toward a most unexpected direction, where, in moments of my greatest challenges, I stood shocked in the realization that the answers were inside of me all the time, patiently waiting for my recognition.

The primary shock was finding that the answers to my problems had actually been hidden in plain sight all the time, waiting to become aware. This awakened in me the turmoil and the peace at the same time. I was astounded to discover that the thing that had come to free me was actually the same thing that could have destroyed me as well. My journey into the unknown began by exploring the endless possibilities that lie within each one of us. I did not come to realize everything just by my own apprehension, though. I was a real self-help junkie, a bit on the edge of societal expectations, dependent on the wisdom from books. Many times it seemed as if they carried the message that I sought after for decades. Once again, life lessons appear in the form most suitable for the pupil at hand.

When I discovered that the good and the bad—as we like to refer to it—lived side by side inside of me and manifested so perfectly on the outside, it was easier to take the past for what it really was: a lesson on life.

I had to let go of many things since then.

Once the weight was off my shoulders, new messages came through my cleared mind.

"Come home, I've been waiting for you ever since you left!"

My dad had said that to me some time ago over the phone, and even though it had been at least thirty years late, it was honest, and it made me recall some past memories with a different type of sadness.

I thought about the many messages gone by just because I was not ready to hear them. How much less horrid the world seems when we open our hearts! When we are willing to stop and listen to the silence, the message it brings often surpasses all our expectations. A moment that either comes or does not come in our life depends upon one condition only—that we are ready for it. And so we grow to higher levels of consciousness; we are never the same within that growth caused by the variety of life situations.

The fact of the matter is that parenting is not just tending to the needs of the body, accumulating knowledge, or dealing with emotions and the expectations of society. It is also tending to the needs of the soul, which is so often bypassed or forgotten. It is a pity that we are not taught in school to recognize the power that hides within us, of life, which is a dance of joy and sorrow and all the opposites that we can ever imagine. They exist only so that we can experience them.

Would this knowledge make life more worth living?

Could we embrace sadness if we knew that it is just an insight into joy?

Could we appreciate the silence and the clamor as well?

Could we recognize the significance of darkness, knowing that it preceded light?

Good intentions and desires are not enough. It is necessary to act.

I see my parents from another perspective now and perceive what my mind had not seen before. I see my aging father, his smile and wide-open eyes resembling those of a small, sincere, inquisitive child. Why did I not notice that before, the peace that he, in his modesty, had spread around to others? And I see my mother, with deep lines crossing her pale face, standing like a rock, defying time, powerful and strong, not giving up. I remember my aunt Maria and the life story of her constant losses. I remember the love and dedication with which she served as a pediatrician. I remember all that with love, and I think how a part of each one of them is a part of me too that I have yet to reveal to myself.

We find the highest values when we close our eyes and dare to take a look inside.

If someone were to ask me whether I would live my life again, I'd say, "No, thank you." However, if you were to ask me whether or not my life was worth living, I would respond lovingly.

I have learned that it is wise to accept both the good and bad in life. Take the good with gratitude, nourish it with love, and spread it to others. The very thing that bothers you most, that which makes you angry and despaired, that which you oppose—accept courageously and embrace, because just like the beautiful things in life, it is a part of you that, if you wish to alter, you must first recognize within. In order to grow, you must be willing to change.

"Surrender is learning to get out of the way of what wants to happen naturally."

—Penney Peirce

About Brothers and Sisters

"Blood is thicker than water."

—Folk saying

I was only ten years old when I left Croatia. As I was ready to leave home, and once the farewells were done, the morning trip to the city proved to be a new experience for me, because my mother, as it had turned out, had taken me on my first shopping spree. But, it was a special occasion indeed. By the end of the morning, rushing from one small shop to another, I was dressed in shades of green, with the exception of a coffee-brown sweater that even for the awe, I remember thinking, *How can my parents afford all this?* Unaccustomed to having anything new to wear, I remember that I could not tear myself away from feeling the importance of the occasion. Not that otherwise we had much to wear, but mostly our clothes were hand-me-downs that our mother, with tremendous effort, transformed into clean and neat outfits.

"Even though it's not new," she would say as she would neatly sew a tear, "it doesn't mean that it should be shabby and torn."

Our father, on the other hand, invested all of his effort just to keep us together and fed, and I imagine it was not easy—ten mouths to feed with one fisherman's salary, but still, even if we were eager, we were not hungry. The rare chocolate bars were always divided into five equal parts, and it was only for St. Nicolas's day that we would each get a whole treat.

I remember how our father insisted that everyone be home in time for lunch. The family lunches were and remain sanctified for him. No one could start eating until we were all seated. We were a big family: five children and five adults, so we could not all fit at one table. Our father made a smaller one for the children to sit next to the elderly. Maria, the oldest child, sat poised above the younger four, making sure order was preserved at the table, an outstretched hand of our mother. I usually sat beside her, babbling about everything I might have found interesting. Anka, two years younger than me, was always quiet with her Mona Lisa smile ready across a beautiful pale face. Svetka, the youngest sister, was somewhat a rebel at large, but her mission was to make life easier, and she always took advantage of the merry side of life. Mario, the youngest one and the long-awaited male child of the family, was a dark-haired, big-eyed three-year-old when I was headed for the States. I've never really had the chance to meet him more closely.

It was after the blessings and after making the sign of the cross that lunch could begin. I remember—although I cannot say that I quite understood—my father as he would hum: "I am a rich man. My riches are my children." He seemed so content that we never doubted his merry statement.

Our mother was, and still is, a very willful and proud woman. She had never been coddled in life, and it left a mark on her and her children as well, as she sternly expected obedience with no questions asked. Despite the fact that we were so numerous, we were always well-mannered and obedient. Work ethics were our mom's teachings, and she allowed no idleness. Our mother insisted that we all help out at home, and our chores were no small matter, which we were sometimes prone to avoid. Often we had quietly complained because there were days when we had to rise in the morning before dawn; unlike our peers, who had the privilege to oversleep, we had chores to do. Nonetheless, we had the opportunity to experience the fullness of life as many others hadn't.

In the early summer mornings, while it was still dark outside, my older sister and I, accompanied by our mother, walked to the vineyards, dragging our feet for more than an hour, and stumbled sometimes, smitten by sleepiness. We would liven up with the dawning of the day. Running along, avoiding rocks, we would race to the second peak of a hill that stood in front of us, fascinated by the expanse that outstretched in front of our eyes. "Mom, is that Italy?" We would nag her for an answer. Straining our eyes in a struggle to see even further, we'd hope for a clear morning when the outlines of a distant land had sometimes been clearly displayed. And then, after the awe that had filled the cells of our soul, we would often suddenly accelerate into a run down the hill. Despite warnings from our mother, we'd come to the vineyard in a gallop before her. In the hours that followed in silence, with only occasional quiet chatter, we pulled the grass from the ground while the sun penetrated and sent fiery rays into our eyes. It was a welcomed sign to return home.

As if we were suddenly awakened, neither the sun nor our mother nor the fear of snakes could have stopped us, while we rolled in high grass, lying on the ground side by side, legs outstretched, arms along the body, we swirled screaming with joy. The once-tall grass was left lying as a witness to our morning madness. And then, even more vigorously, we ran in front of Mother to come home, while the other children still slept, tired and sweaty. We often jumped into the seawater to wash out the dirt and grass; there was an enormous amount of relief, followed by remission of tension. And fulfillment came at last, as we would throw ourselves onto our beds to compensate for lost sleep.

Even upon first glance, one could easily notice the difference in our looks and character, but as befits brothers and sisters, we did have a thing or two in common: two reddish-haired sisters, two chocolaty-brown, and the brother's dark hair highlighted blond by the summer sun. Except for our brother, we were all pale-faced like our mother. Not that I cared much for looks, but I was always fascinated by my older sister Maria and her red, fluffy curls which, since I could remember, reached to the middle of her back. Although a bit shy and delicate, with freckles all over her face, she was steady as a rock, and in my life, she was often the pillar I could lean against and rely on. Her strength was not so much in the words that she spoke, because she was never able to outspeak me, but she stood strong in the silence that was clearer than words. It was the silence that said, "I'm here for you."

I do not know why it is so, because after many years of change, turmoil, and searching, falling and rising, she is still here. She still is a little shy and timid, still knows how to listen, and she is still a pillar one can lean and rely on.

I have read many books about the elements of success in life, and there has often been a mention of that one person believing in you. If that is so, then she is the one for me who had made the difference, my older sister Maria. Even though I was the one, just a year younger, who was more outreaching, the one who went away, saw the world and went to college, she remained wise, always set on being kind, thoughtful, and fair.

It makes me think: you don't have to be rich, well-known, highly educated, or look like a star, and yet you can be special to that one person at least, and it makes a big difference in that someone's life. Sometimes even the smallest things matter, and you never know what those might be. And as much as hurt clings to the heart, so does an honest and warm gesture, especially when it comes from those we love.

> *"An older sister is a friend and defender, a conspirator, a counselor and a sharer of delights. And sorrows too."*
>
> **—Pam Brown**

Friends Forever

"When I write letters to you, thoughts just keep coming and never cease to end. So many concerns and I have to create fences, those iron hard barriers. If I'm boring you, it might be less cruel if you come to see and believe that the letters to you are windows into my soul, my book of life, attempts 'to define along the way,' a relief but also a burden because they open up a series of new questions that require a response and the response consumes time. It's six o'clock, my books are open on the table and I smell flowers, tired legs out stretched press against my sleepy eyes.

". . . I find comfort in you, my poems and books.

Lots of love,

Tamara"

—Excerpt from a letter, April 15, 1988

It was September 1984. I had just turned seventeen and had returned to Croatia. In September, I was the thirty-first consecutive junior attendee in a class of a prominent high school in the city of Zadar. Seemingly confident, decisive, but inwardly insecure and somewhat shy, I was seated in the first bench of the middle row, waiting for the mention of my name to be presented to new classmates. My heart was pounding wildly, threatening to take my breath away when, out of the corner of my eye, I caught sight of an eloquent apparition in the third row, next to the wall.

"My God!" I sighed. "If I could just as smoothly glide words from my lips as she does . . ."

I decided to meet her; she said her name was Tamara. The rest is a part of my twenty-year-old history often defined by letters, written at a time when we were separated by attending different colleges and pursuing life in different directions.

> *"I am missing our wanderings after school,*
>
> *Rainy evenings,*
>
> *The cookies and one glove,*
>
> *The sea gulls, conversations and the silence . . .*
>
> *The extravagance and Donat ice creams in warm summer days . . .*
>
> *The walks and benches, and minus A's, plus B's and F's.*
>
> *I'm missing the last row seats,*
>
> *The hole in the door,*
>
> *Intentional and 'unintentional' ditching,*

Good Bilusic, our Babinka and Jasenka and Ana (I dreamed her last night).

I'm missing expectation—

Second legs in the row.

(I know I know what you will say now. I don't live in the past, there will be more nice things, but don't be angry, these are just fond memories.)

Missing dearest friend,

True love and trust in myself that has now gone astray . . .

Post cards with ships and sails,

Missing our Pegula.

Love,

Tamara"

—Excerpt from a letter, April 15, 1988

It's hard to say what would have happened if I hadn't found the courage to introduce myself to the world called Tamara. In the next twenty years of our encounters, she was an inherent part of me—one soul in two bodies, as Aristotle said. We laughed and cried together, studied and learned, dreamed and made plans, mourned when it didn't turn out the way we had wanted it to; we shared our clothes, our secrets, and our hopes, as well.

Not that we were so similar one to another; rather, we were like two sides of the same coin, like opposites that somehow perfectly matched. Something held us together like glue, inseparable even when distance and people defied us to split. I wonder if it weren't maybe the desire placed in a common interval of being, connecting two souls into one that requested the same: the innocence of love. It seemed that our worlds were parallel, only versions of opposites. And it's clear that we had not met by chance.

However, as time passes and distance dilutes memories, while life's congestion casts a shadow on the meaning, how easy it is to forget! In the busy flow of life, in moments when we are overwhelmed with work, it is a magical feeling when the meaning re-appears. We often seek hints of truths, staring at meaningless articulations of what was or what should have been. We criticize and gossip, unaware of the truth that has already been imposed.

"Look inside," the wind whispers, but we turn to external fixations we tend to call reality, that which it is not. Casually and spontaneously, in the years that have passed by, even though we rarely see each other anymore, I remember what my time with Tamara has taught me:

Friends are people you can rely on in the hardest of times.

A friend holds your hand while you grow stronger and then thrusts you into the world, so that you can find the pillar of strength in yourself.

We carry our friends in our hearts, no matter where we are or where they might be.

"A friend is one that knows you as you are, understands where you have been, accepts what you have become, and still, gently allows you to grow."

—William Shakespeare

The Choices We Make

When I turned eighteen, I remember how exceedingly angry I was with my cousin, who—in good faith, I'm sure—on account of my shattered relationship with Aunt Maria, told me: "Do as you like, but remember, we are all blacksmiths of our own happiness!"

I was so angry with my cousin that I burst out and really wanted to hurt him back. But it brought no consolation, just the lingering of his words throughout the next few years. He may not have thought about it later, as I had, but the words had carved themselves into my mind permanently. I have a feeling today that he meant no harm, just wanted to imply that I was wasting my chances and what had hit me the most was, in fact, the truth behind the words: the hint of the power within myself to make that change which would satisfy my needs. Astonishingly enough, I had wasted both at the time. I neither had the opportunity anymore nor the education that I had desired, and I wasn't happy either. To imply that I could somehow be responsible for my own happiness seemed to be the overstatement of the year. Behind all that anger, I couldn't recognize the truth, even when it had hit me.

When I was ten years old, they asked me, "Do you want to go to America?"

"Yes," I replied joyfully and without giving it much thought. And I went.

When I wanted to come home after the first month, I did not understand why I could not.

So when is a choice a choice?

I've noticed over time that when the question is imposed upon a small child, a requirement of choice, the child always chooses in the now. She tends to her most urgent needs. The child chooses to be happy, and when she fails to be, she asks: "Why not?"

As we grow, we develop our logic and tend to believe that we are capable, almost with mathematical precision, to predict the outcomes of our choices. For example, I believe that my parents had their best interest at heart when they decided to give me away, believing that I would get the best education provided and a chance for a better life. The only things that they could not predict were the details of the outcome of their decision. They could not predict the choices that I myself would make.

Based upon our experiences and the choices that we have made in the past, at one time or another, it all boils down to our ability to analyze the if-then conditions. Things get tricky when the accumulated experiences begin to align, and we start treating choices for good or bad, depending on whether they have caused pleasure or discomfort in the past. One could say that at some point in life, we choose in the past.

I am convinced that we are very conscious beings at the moment of birth, faced with the biggest challenge of all—to keep the memory of who we are alive as we grow. However, as we are born totally physically limited and dependent upon others, we slowly start to turn our focus outward, and the memory of our consciousness slowly fades to a complete amnesia. At some point, largely due to the fact that we live at an accelerated pace in a society with great external requirements, we basically become the physical body that thinks and feels.

The idea of "I think, therefore I am" powered my mind for quite a long time. For many years, I remained a prisoner of the intellect, counting on it as my biggest asset. I believed that it was my strongest ally until the moment I realized that it was to become my biggest weakness. When I think about it now, I remember my son, Frane, who, even as a child, frowned at the mere mention of IQ, not to forget his displeasure at my applauding the analytical mind. The grown-ups often tell their children, "You'll understand when you grow up!" The truth is too often radically opposed. Only some individuals can acquire the insight that was there when they were small children.

In the following phase of my personal quest, I believed: "I feel, therefore I am real." Even at an early age, I was inclined to tumultuous emotions. It seemed sometimes that my emotions went from one extreme to another in just a few seconds. Everything, absolutely everything, had burst with a strong emotional charge. At first, there were shorter periods, and then they started to get longer, until eventually I was stuck in despair. I remained there for a good ten years.

I do not know exactly what effects the regaining of consciousness but readiness is certainly a prime factor. We are witnesses each, as we daily observe people around us, that if awareness doesn't arrive, the body begins to fail rapidly and often dies far more prematurely than one would ever predict.

I believe that birth is a choice.

Even as children, we make choices that affect our lives.

Choice is the first sign of freedom.

Choice means that we have at least two options between which we can choose.

The choice can be conscious or unconscious, but it is still a choice.

The choices can make us happy or unhappy, but they are still choices nevertheless.

Each choice, whether or not we consider it right or wrong, teaches us something.

Just like children, we learn from wrong choices.

It is up to us, though, whether or not we will.

Having been given the freedom of choice and that of making mistakes too, it is not always easy to make up one's mind. Afraid of other people's opinions, we often misuse that freedom and impose it upon others as blame. The burden of choice might be easier if we could ask ourselves:

What is it that attracts my attention without excess analysis?

What *feels* right?

We might be surprised to find that the obvious choice might not always be that which seems reasonable and generally acceptable at first. It might even imply a radical change and coping with the present fears. We are prone to avoid what frightens us somehow, but that might just be a good place to start. Perhaps it would imply a sort of waking up from a dream in which our current choices were conditioned in every imaginable and unimaginable way. Perhaps it would be a sort of awakening of the consciousness that was lost somewhere. If current choices do not make us happy, maybe it's time to move on. Choose again.

Wouldn't it be nice if we could ask Tesla or Edison why they played with electricity when it could have killed them? It would be nice if we could ask Charlie Chaplin why he still entertained in his style when he was repeatedly refused in Hollywood. It would be interesting to find out how Darwin became a successful scientist when his interest was supported by neither his parents nor his teachers. What if Einstein had given up exploring the world when he was expelled from school? What if Disney had believed in his own incompetence when he was laid off from work due to "lack of imagination"?

The answer lies within the freedom of choice.

I am sure that they all chose to do things that felt right, things they personally believed in and complied with happiness, even when others believed otherwise. Following their gut feeling, they did not need to rationalize or justify their choices to others. They chose for themselves, but that choice ultimately made many others happy and contributed to the world as well.

It's not easy today to find the right job or field of work, but the same principles can be applied. We can always ask ourselves:

What made me happy when I was a child?

What did I want to be or do or have?

How is it different from what I have now?

Finally: the time that fits into the space between birth and death is the sum of all choices. No matter how hard we try, we can never know the exact outcome of it. We can fool ourselves and anticipate all possibilities, but the result is not within our grasp. It's a delusion to even think that we can plan everything. Sometimes things turn out worse, but sometimes things turn out better than ever expected. So, what if we choose wrong? It is not the end of time, just a step closer to a new choice to make. Every day is about making choices. That's how we learn and make ourselves better. But we need faith.

When we abandon the need to control everything in our lives, we realize that life shows forth the unstoppable magic of creation and that every choice, even one that seems like a failure, is valuable and unique. When we realize that the time available to us is a choice, we might in our morning hurry to work, stop for a moment—perhaps for the first time—to hear the chirping of the birds and ask ourselves, "Have they sung before?"

Whether we believe that the choices are ours to make or that they are not—either way, we are right.

> *"I won't tell you that the world matters nothing, or the world's voice, or the voice of society. They matter a good deal. They matter far too much. But there are moments when one has to choose between living one's own life, fully, entirely, completely—*

or dragging out some false, shallow, degrading existence that the world in its hypocrisy demands. You have that moment now. Choose!"

—Oscar Wilde

Faith

I am quite sure that my mother still fears for me. She often asks, "Do you pray, Vesna?"

I hold no hard feelings, because she, in good faith, cares for me and prays to God that I may one day be received into His kingdom.

"No, Mom," I answer for the hundredth time, not wanting to explain again. "I know that you pray for me."

"Aren't you afraid?" she timidly inquires, because she knows that I do not appreciate her asking me repeatedly.

"No, Mom," I say tersely, knowing that she will ask again.

Ever since my sisters, my brother and I were able to walk, on Sunday mornings we would always go to church. Accompanied by our parents and grandparents as well, for as long as they could, we would put on our best attire and go to church for Mass. Like other children, I was often bored, and when the crowd was larger for big church holidays, we would crouch behind the old church organ, away from everyone's view, and when no one observed, we played a guessing game with our coins.

As I had learned to read at an early age, my parents and our pastor pushed me, along with some older children, into the first row, next to the altar. I was soon well known for my readings of the epistles. I rejoiced, for it had killed the boredom. Not that I understood everything I read, but I soon began to be tremendously attracted by the view from the altar. With every sigh from the back of the church, where the older ladies with their bent backs would sit, I would get an incentive, which prompted me to highlight a word, to rest at a comma, and to make a full stop at each period. In the seconds that were in the pauses between the spoken words, I saw those faces, listening with great attention, and my view would remain awhile in the grooves on the dark faces that were wrapped in black scarves, which testified about a time I did not get to know. Eventually I was able to embrace all faces in one that connected into a single image and quietly spoke of untold fear and suffering.

When I went to America, my aunt Maria, who was aware of my early Christian upbringing at home, enrolled me in a local Catholic school. Every Sunday, we were expected to attend Mass. Not that I liked to go, but since I already had to, I sat near the choir, which roared loudly, accompanied by keyboards and guitar. Sometimes I felt as if I were at a concert and not in a church.

Is this even allowed? I wondered.

Before long, I began to avoid going to Mass, and as long as Aunt Maria was sending envelopes with dollars, no one bothered me. When not attending Mass became a habit, sometime in the middle of my seventh-grade year, I asked my aunt to transfer me to a local public school, and she agreed, having noticed my lack of interest in the sacred. So it happened that I, though born and brought up in a strict Christian spirit, at the age of thirteen entered a less-familiar territory, which in the years that followed, I carefully investigated.

I still went to church sometimes, mostly for major holidays, and still as a habit, although I must admit, there was little consolation to be found there. I was attracted to the peace and quiet of my room, finding a safe haven away from crowds of people. Not finding any consolation within organized religion, still I felt secure enough with a different kind of faith, which I could not then define. For years, "the feeling of faith" has been my loyal companion, and a guide at times, that something in me that has never left me since, that something that I still have difficulty explaining to my determined mom.

> "*I believe in intuitions and inspirations . . .*
> *I sometimes* feel *that I am right. I do not* know *that*
> *I am.*"

> **—Albert Einstein**

PART TWO

To Love Is to Change: Light at the End of the Corridor

"The privilege of living is to be your own."

—Joseph Campbell

People tell me that I amaze with my sudden decisions. Interestingly enough, I believe the truth to be quite the contrary. Although to an observer, it may often seem like a sharp turn, for me it has always been just one clear-cut decision after a period of smoldering and maturation. The same happened when I decided to leap forward toward a new life in Zadar.

It was fifteen years ago, and I am certain that it had been the beginning of the death of one of my identities and the birth of another. In the first months of this period of my life, my second son, Mario, was born. Along with the ten-year-old Frane, we dared step boldly into the unknown—I because of my own determination, and they because of my choices. I chose not to listen to the whispered rumors, the criticism, and the forecasts, but rather to my own heart. I knew I had to make radical changes in my life. I knew that it wasn't going to be easy. I knew I had to endure, but I had wanted it so badly that it wasn't just a matter of choice anymore; it was a matter of survival. I felt lifeless on the inside—the passion for life gone. But even then, when everything seemed to crumble and plunge, there still lay a possibility of choice of making a meaningful transformation. Of course, change is hard on everyone, because it implies that we break free from old, destructive thoughts, feelings, and actions. But it is quite necessary nevertheless.

There comes a time in the life of every individual, one lucid moment when you know exactly what you have to do. It is usually not what you would do in your "sound mind"; it is not something that meets the general approval of the public, and it is not always the easiest way out, but it is something inside pushing you to act, and you are not at ease until you do. If you turn your attention away and ignore it, you might just miss the one break you have been waiting for all your life.

The best opportunities are not always packaged in cellophane. Neither was mine.

I decided to take the plunge. I learned to say no to the things that I didn't want. The nos were often followed by confrontation, and the hardest ones were within me and my family. The more nos I said, the less support I seemed to have gotten, until at the end, I was quite alone in my determination, but still I grew stronger. I had, at the time, left a steady career in school, left the island, Dugi otok, and went on to look for employment in the city. I searched for anything just to survive. I finally landed a job in a company seeking someone fluent in English. I barely had enough money to pay the nanny with the initial income, let alone the food and bills, but I had my mind set and my heart into it, and I soon started to earn more money than I ever had at school. As I progressed at work, more responsibilities involving managing certain segments of the company arose, and my workload spread rapidly, so I soon began to travel throughout Europe and farther still.

It was a very vibrant time of my life, with quite a workload to handle—two young children to take care of, the frequent changes of residence and nannies—but we made it work somehow. It was an era when I had probably learned the most about life. Being responsible for many people in the company, I had to learn a lot about human relations, but primarily I had to learn about myself, and I went on to develop on a personal level. On top of business, management, and marketing, I also learned about active listening, forgiveness, meditation, relaxation, and release. I learned from all possible available sources: from books, from my superiors, colleagues, and acquaintances in Croatia and beyond. Everything and everyone became a potential learning experience, and I was eager and ready to learn. I was insatiable and ready for the change. It seemed as if I was compensating for all the passive years that had been lost forever.

New worlds began to evolve. Everything had completely changed—the circumstances of my life, my world as I knew it, and me as well. I was a totally new person who met different people on a daily basis and lived an entirely new and different life from the one I had known before. It was a resurrection from the deadness that had grown on me for decades. A total transformation began to unfold in the mind, body, and soul as well, but it was not always an easy mission to follow. My biggest challenge were my children who, like me, were undergoing a complete reconstruction of their lives in the uproar of emotions. This was particularly apparent with the older son,

Frane, who, accustomed to life in the country and because of my divorce, seemed to have suffered the most. Mario, on the other hand, even at birth, was a completely different child. He seemed unburdened and joyful; he bore the seed of delight that followed him wherever he moved. He brought much-needed hope, warmth, and harmony to our home.

In the years that followed, I began to strengthen as a person, but also financially and socially as well. Although I believed in myself and was determined to provide for my children, I still longed for much-needed compassion and love.

Gradually, I grew content in the love given and received by my children, and it began to take shape and come back into my life multiplied. I began to receive approval where there was none before; I met wonderful people I had not noticed earlier. Unlike the previous years, when I was a magnet for disaster, I was now drawn to some different energy and some different populace. From my changes inside, the transformation had sprung up and manifested externally. Some people vanished from my life and were gone for good. Some new ones entered silently and unexpectedly, with the appearance of an unusual soul mate who had forever marked my knowledge of the unknown. Some came to stay for the ride. It's as if I finally began to receive the anticipated love of decades before, and it was at a time when I least expected it. When I was peaceful at heart, all came effortlessly and naturally.

There is no guarantee that we will one day awaken in life and begin its transformation. No one can help us if we are cloistered to change. Whether we believe that there is darkness or light at the end of the hallway, either way, we are right. It is what we believe that shapes our lives. We decide. We choose, and we initiate change.

The Love Within

What Is Love?

> *"Flowers, trees and branches."* —*Vito (age 5)*

> *"Friendship."* —*Lea (age 6)*

> *"Spring, when the flowers bloom."* —*Cvita (age 4)*

> *"Swinging together."* —*Sara (age 4)*

> *"When we love each other."* —*Kim (age 6)*

> *"When I go to the park and play with Mom."* —*Ira (age 4)*

> *"Love is everlasting."* —*Giovanni (age 6)*

> **—*Zadar, Svarozic Day Care Center,***
> ***February 11, 2009***

It is interesting to find that as we grow up, the word *love* is almost exclusively linked to that found in a relationship between a man and a woman. What is it that happens to shape our thoughts so that we are able to perceive love's other shapes? As the memory of the growing years fades, experiences pile up, only to become selective and exclusive. Children, without excess information on their minds, see love everywhere: in a friend, an animal, a tree, and the cycle of change—in every respect. If we were to ask all children the significance of the word *love* and then gather the answers, I am sure that ultimately, the meaning would involve the entire universe. It is an amazing fact, one that further implies that children know much more than they are able to express. Why? Because children do not need to prove *what is;* they simply *are.* Of course, in the eye of a nescient observer, they leave the impression of unawareness, due to their simplicity and the obvious lack of experience.

I had never thought about love much until I was totally lost in its absence. For a long time, the meaning of the word *love* was a cliché to me, but its secrets began to unravel slowly when I started my search for love inside of me. While I uncovered bits and pieces of what seemed like hidden riches, I began to realize that I was actually exposing my unconscious self to my conscious self. Beneath the layered surface, beneath the anger, fear, and disappointment, I came upon some radiance, reflections long forgotten. In times of solitude, alone with myself, I could often feel some odd connection, a spark smoldering that had threatened to escalate into something more. I was surprised when I discovered that deep within, love squatted and waited for its moment of illumination, unwearyingly and peacefully, as if buried in infinity. I was afraid at first, because I thought that if I gave it too much significance, it might alter or vanish. During the timid but persistent journeys to my inside, I was able to rule out fear and regain self-confidence. I had nothing to lose and everything to gain. All the while, before, I had looked for love everywhere but within, and the second I chose to notice it, somehow it started to find me on the outside too.

I began to feel love, and it was not related to any particular person; yet it was associated with everyone all at once. I started to feel a strange connection with others. I could sometimes identify and feel a tie with everything around me, and in moments of such blessings, I felt that I was not alone, that there was still much to uncover, that reality was just beginning to dawn on me, and that it reflected my dare to change in life. It seemed as if I had just awakened from sleep and begun living. The misconception that love belongs in a remote place enshrined by a human appearance slowly left my body and my thoughts as well. I knew I was finally greeting what had begun to develop deep within. I felt love, and it dwelled. I felt the good in others, even when they themselves did not. I knew that I could be considerate and supportive of others too, but at the same time, I was beginning to become aware that everyone had to find this truth for themselves, *in* themselves. No one can inflict change on another, least of all by force.

When we open our hearts, when we expose it—even if it means that it might be wounded—we open it to love. Not to open our hearts means depriving ourselves of the experience of giving and receiving. If we do not give unconditionally, we get nothing—nothing that is worth keeping.

Therefore, at a turning point in my life, I began to discover that everything dwelled in me, and there was nothing out there that could not be found inside of me. I found out that the world was my mirror; it reflected my willingness to give honestly and unconditionally. As I left the old beliefs behind, when I no longer had a need for them, my life accelerated at high speed, and magic started to happen. I felt support, but

I knew that it was in me. I felt joy, but I knew that it was a reflection of my new self. I felt love, and it overwhelmed me.

There is nothing to find externally while we dare not look for it inside. We cannot see in others that which we cannot find in ourselves first.

I began to believe with all my heart that there is a love that is everlasting, even if it is changeable. We do not have to know everything about it, because it is mysterious; it plays a game of hide-and-seek—sometimes it's there, and sometimes it's hidden, but never estranged. In the game of letting go, I had encountered expressions of love where I least expected it. In the years that have passed, I realized that to love unconditionally means to be willing to let go. To love unconditionally means not to claim or be claimed. I learned not to judge what I didn't understand. I learned otherwise, noted and accepted that there are different types of love, and like everything else in this world, one love does not resemble another on the outside. But in its essence, it's the same—good, flexible, and unquestionable. I have learned in the last ten years that love has no rules. Love is the bond between beings whose souls are linked at a deeper level than the one we see in plain sight. Love is never tiresome. It's a flicker of light, bright and bendable.

When I decided to end my ten-year marriage, I was overwhelmed with thoughts of doubt. The fears of the accumulated years of listening to criticism bubbled to the surface: "You will not succeed . . . To destroy the marriage will bring back luck . . . You'll destroy your children, and you will bear the guilty for that." There seemed to be all sorts of valid reasons to stay put, but despite it, I went on to listen to the weak voice of my own heart. The many advice suppliers I had resented then spoke out of the possibilities of their own mind.

They had good intent but were hidden under their own fright, in which they were wrapped and unaware. They also spoke as if mirrored by my own uncertainties. The more conscious I became of my own feelings, the more I was able to notice the reflections in others. As for me, I knew I had to make that step forward, the step into the unknown, which came to seem far safer than staying in the familiar.

Fifteen years have passed since then, and if I hadn't finally dared do what I had feared the most, I would never have learned about the world I now live in. I had a choice to make. I had to confront my fears and step out of the world that had grown on me like a weed. Even though the process was painful, it was simultaneously beautiful in the exposure of things I had learned.

I now enjoy knowing that absolutely everything—happiness and disaster, love and hate, and all possible opposites—are a fundamental part of me, just as they are a part of the whole universe. The universe is a dance of opposites. To embrace this game of opposites is to enjoy life. I found love not when I needed it most or when I searched for it desperately, but at a time when I decided to *let life be* and turned to myself. It was only then that love manifested itself externally in abundance. When I found the support within myself, it glowed in others as well.

The search for the external does not help us find that which lies within.

Today I enjoy a beautiful manifestation of love. There is no need to adapt my love to anyone's. Regardless of any external circumstances, I know that the last ten years have been worthier than I have ever been ready to expect. Letting go brings peace to the heart. In this surrender, there is a possibility of failure, but I'm no longer afraid, because I know where the source is.

My mother once said (and has probably long forgotten it since): "Vesna, you're a good person." Maybe she has forgotten because she doesn't praise easily; but I haven't, because those words bore witness of my change. When I was ready to be taught, when I found myself in love with life itself, when I became satisfied with just a day's work, when I no longer had the need to blame others for their convictions, it showed externally too. Whether we like it or not, we emit subtle but powerful vibrations around us, and anyone with whom we come in contact quickly picks up these vibrations, whether it is joy or fear, jealousy or love. It's not the words but the vibrations that we eventually absorb. I know the feeling in situations when people try to convince me of something but fail. We don't need words to express feelings; we are able to touch the hearts of everyone we meet, even if only in passing, while waiting our turn at the dentist, in a bakery or a store. No one is completely separated from another being, thing, or phenomenon; we all participate in this cosmic dance of love, but the personal manifestations that we encounter are our interpretations and not the truth itself.

> *"Love is not a matter of what happens in life. It's a matter of what's happening in your heart."*
>
> **—Ken Keyes**

Those Divine Children

"Unlike grownups, children have little need to deceive themselves."

—Johann Wolfgang von Goethe

Children are an inexhaustible source of inspiration. They truly reflect love, joy, sincere curiosity, and despite their apparent lack of experience, wisdom as well. On many occasions, it seems that I have learned more from them than they have from me.

My five-year-old daughter, Sara, and most of the rest of the family were engaged in watching a TV show when she popped the question open: "Mommy, Mommy . . ." She was persistent as she pulled my sleeve. "Why do we exist?"

Even having given the question some thought in the past, it came abruptly and when I had least expected it. Such a direct question required a direct answer, and I was a bit insecure how to respond. "Well, I think we exist so as to perceive the beauty of this world." I finally said out loud.

"You think?" she blasted, astonished. "You're not even sure!" Obviously she was disappointed.

"Sara . . ." I began, "it is a life's mission finding the answer to that question . . ."

"And did you find it?" she suddenly interrupted my flow of thoughts.

A bit of shame came to possess me, as the question was left hanging in the air, and her attention was drawn again to that of the television show. I was left stunned by the unspoken response, as if stripped naked by what had been imposed. My thoughts disconnected from what was happening around me in an inevitable self-confrontation. I had to admit that I did not know the answer. Not that I didn't search for it and wonder, but I was just never as directly confronted with the reality of the question as on that day, to ever conclusively sum up my thoughts. It had cast me into a more intensive search for the answer, to that within. Meanwhile, Sara reminded me daily by inquiring, "Have you found your answer?" It was a bit annoying to have a child pressure you into finding an answer and not vice versa.

By that time I was self-employed and worked long hours in my day care center. It was only after a few meaningful and dedicated years of working with small children that the issue that had questioned the further financial existence of the center began to arise. My own goals did not agree with policies of the local politicians. It was a matter of quantity over quality that had finally shattered my dreams of making the difference in preschool education.

"What am I missing?" The question began to preoccupy me even more than it ever had before. The dedicated hours of work, the commitment to achieve the best, the work that had manifested in the satisfaction of parents and children equally still did not seem to be enough for us to succeed financially. I had a terrible feeling of missing something for a long time, but then it hit me.

I had felt for some time that there was a greater purpose for my visit to Earth, to the here and now, but its meaning had always eluded me before. I searched for an answer, but instead it had found me. Working with children, I had indeed encountered vast quantities of inspiration and joy, but that was not the purpose of the day care center. I have learned, and feel a certainty, that my mission was very plain—to play once more, even if it only lasted for a few years—but those were the few years that had made all the difference in my life. I was able to get in touch with the long-lost child within myself, to hear its cries and mend its wounds. Despite my decision to close up shop, and despite the seemed "failure" to achieve set goals, there came a time to sit down and count the losses but also the victories as well. We can learn from every situation, and it was mine to learn from children. When I had learned the lesson well, it was time again to close up shop and move on. After five years of paying attention, the always-dazzling children, the crowds of people who have passed the hallways, new friends and acquaintances, working as a team, I closed the day care center. It was something I had thought would last a very long time when, in fact, it lasted only long enough for me to learn.

People often ask, "It didn't work?" more as a stale statement than a question. Some assume that I had failed, but I now have a different definition of failure than most people. Some still nostalgically recall the vibrancy that has reigned in the hearts of all those who were touched; some do not understand, and some never will. And I know the truth, for it prevails. My heart has stored a memory of the pure and uncorrupted children who have encouraged my finding myself, and I know that they had not come by chance, because I finally found what I had sought after—the glimmer of peace itself. It encouraged me to revive the child inside who was lost long ago, the one who had known to look forward to little things, the one who could recognize the miraculous within the ordinary, the one who could be happy and look ahead without cause, the one who knew the secret of life but had forgotten it with time. I recall with affection, and I thank each and every child who will perhaps one day recognize himself in this narrative, because I was touched to the depths of my soul, exposed, and enlightened.

Sara has always been very inquisitive and has never made parenthood easier. She seemed to have been most inspired in the evenings as she was getting ready for bed. Delaying sleep, she began to sigh one evening, "How lucky you are, Mom. You know why you exist! How will I ever find that out?"

I didn't want her to trap me into a discussion, but she was so adorable in her intent that I answered mildly, "I've read, studied, and thought about things, made a lot of mistakes, and then I came to some conclusions."

Sara looked at me, obviously pleased that she had managed to start a conversation, and continued undisturbed, "What have you actually learned?"

Hesitating, wondering whether to give an answer to that question or not, I replied cautiously, "I found out that we are in this world to find the real self . . ."

Sara was obviously discouraged by the indistinct answer, but I deliberately did not explain further. I could see within her eyes the attempt to place the answer in her acceptable framework. After a short silence, she asked, "And what if I find out something else?"

"Then it will be *your* understanding of life," I confirmed.

"Well, then I will read a lot too." She concluded the interview temporarily, and satisfied with the answer, leaned her head on the pillow and closed her eyes to sleep.

Most often, the teachers in our lives are older than we. They have more knowledge and wisdom gained by life, but I've learned that teachers come in the form of small children too, who lecture us with amazing simplicity. Like I said before, the lessons in life seem to come to a form most suitable to its pupil. Often I learned, and I still learn from our children, Sara, Mario, Alan, and Frane—but also from other children I have encountered throughout time; they have taught me that life is worth living, that every moment of every day is a blessing you can take pleasure in. I have learned that happiness dwells in me, and I have learned that magic really exists if you believe in it.

> *"Don't say,"* Sara argued, *"that fairies don't exist! If not here, then definitely on another planet. They do. I'm sure."*

When Mario, my second-born son, was seven years old, for medical reasons then uncertain, what happened to me was one of the most terrifying experiences for a parent: Mario had, for a moment, ceased to breathe. I do not know how long it had taken him to come back, though to me, it seemed like an eternity. The only thing I can recollect of the moment while we waited for the emergency workers to arrive was my calling out to him: "Mario, come back to me!"

When Mario finally opened his eyes in the hospital, he told me a story of what he said was a very stunning dream. I stood in amazement as he talked about how he passed through a long hallway of "tiles" with images of his life displayed in front of him. He told me that he was drawn by a strong light hovering slightly and then moved away from Earth, where he saw Aunt Maria fly by, and others he didn't recognize, and how everything was peaceful and calm. He told me how he had heard my plea and that he was very sorry to see me cry, so he had decided to come back. He told me this as tears ran down my cheeks, and I could no longer focus on the story. I knew that what I had witnessed then was a miracle and that miracles do happen every day in our lives if we are awake enough to notice them. It took me a long time to figure out the message behind it. Affected, in fear that it might happen again, I wasn't open enough for what was obvious.

Mario and I were casually sitting at the kitchen table in our new home a year later, and I do not know how we ever came to talk about death. The only thing I remember was that I was still hesitant in terms of what had happened to Mario. He then comforted me by saying, "Don't be afraid, Mom. And even if I die, I'll always be nearby." I knew right then that the wisdom that came out of his mouth was not that of an eight-year-old boy but that of a much higher intelligence than I was willing to perceive.

I troubled myself about the meaning of "near" for a long time, because I was stunned by the words that had come out of him. I went on to believe that "near" meant in the form of a ghostly figure, but somehow I now feel that *close* is as close as one can get—in the premises of one's own heart.

People, including our children, come into our lives, sometimes to stay a long time and sometimes awhile shorter. We need not fear because of possible separation and because they bind to us tightly. As has been said so many times before—in a change called *life,* the only constant is change itself. If we accept each moment as special, we bring a ray of magic to our lives. Finally, I have given up the desire to control every instant, and I am tranquil enough to realize that everything is already there within us.

When he was eight years old, for the first time, I felt his sadness. Mario came home from school, threw his bag into the corner of his room, and said, "I don't want to go to school anymore!" Concerned, I sat beside him and listened to him while he talked about what had happened in religion class. "My teacher," he began, "wanted to know how I sought God. Initially, I said no, but she insisted, and then I said that God, for me, is not an old man with a gray beard, and that God is for me all the stars and planets and the whole universe. Because of what I said, the children began to make fun of me, and they went on to say that if I did not believe in God, then surely I believed in the devil. I was very miserable and tried to explain, but they all began to talk at once, and I was confused. I have no friends!" he concluded sadly.

"What did your teacher say?" I asked as my heart started to pound harder, because I had asked her not to request Mario to make a stand about his faith. I knew that his thinking was "too mature for his age," as the school psychiatrist had said, and I was afraid that his peers would not understand him, but I could not assume that an adult could be even more irresponsible.

"Nothing," he concluded.

After two days spent in the house and hours and hours of conversation with him, and only a faint intervention at school, I wondered, *Where has the tolerance gone?* And again, with respect to those who obediently go after academic achievement, and with no offense to any religion, my only concern was to restore faith in the heart of a child—the faith that he is worthy, that he is special and loved, and that he has the right to think and feel differently.

It took several weeks, during which we worked together to awaken his shaky self-confidence. Thanks to his blunt and cheerful character, Mario quickly recovered and again took his place in the classroom, long ago leaving behind what had happened.

I must admit that I was very resentful of the apparent clumsiness with which the whole matter was handled in school. However, today I look at it differently, because I know that we are all at various stages of awareness, and we behave accordingly. When we escape from our personal quests, to protect our children at any cost, when we step aside to understand, perhaps we can loosen up. Our children follow their school of life at their own pace learning from all possible resources. It may seem a lack of interest, but it is much more than it appears. The children, like us, learn from their own experience. Trying at all cost to protect them against pain and injury actually slows down their growth, maturity, and progress. Our job as parents, as I see it, is to be there for them and to encourage them on their way.

It's hard to say how much joy Mario introduced to my life but also to the lives of others as well. But we are all equally special, even if we don't recognize it. It's just that we do not distinguish it in ourselves. Everyone has a reason to exist, and in the uniqueness of all of us lies perfection in the fact.

"Mom, I would like to be called Vic (a Croatian word meaning *joke*)!" Mario said determinedly from the door after coming home from school.

"Vic?" I thought, but was not sure about the choice.

"Yes, Vic," he continued. "As a joke, because I love to amuse people. I love it when people smile, when they are happy."

It made sense when he explained it like that. Mario, a fourteen-year-old now, even though he had not changed his name, he hadn't altered what he truly is: a source of joy. Time and again, people stop and say, "I've met your Mario . . ." and I know what they will utter. I do not know what it is in him, but somehow he truly touches the hearts of everyone he meets. Sometimes it seems that people even complain when they say, "Your Mario asks really tough questions. Imagine what he asked me! He asked if me if I'm happy? How do you respond to that?"

I often wonder what makes him different. Is it the child in him that is so vibrant? Although sometimes it seems to me that the child is a wise old man simultaneously.

I ask again: is wisdom not inherent in children?

It was the end of the school year, and Mario was about to finish his eighth year of formal education. I had waited for my turn to talk to his homeroom teacher. Indulged in a conversation with moms who had already waited awhile, chatting about the usual teenage problems, I budged in to comment how it seemed to me that children often naturally recognize what is good for them—only to earn a look of disbelief with words left unsaid between us. How easy it is to marvel when children do exactly what we desire and believe to be correct. But how difficult it is to accept the alternative—when they do otherwise—the possibility that they may instinctively know what is good for them—not that they always follow their own heart (especially as they grow older)! It is a hard blow to a parent's ego that likes control.

My further dialogue with his homeroom teacher didn't go well either, as it seemed that I hadn't reacted "appropriately" to Mario's lonely F for a forgotten homework assignment. I tried to explain—unsuccessfully—that I didn't mind a lonely F if there seemed to be no greater worry behind it. I know that it's popular to measure the amount of success by school grades and achievement. As for me, even if my academic achievements were always above average, and even if I had spent a lot of time working as a teacher, still I cannot understand the emphasis placed on academic achievement, rather than on the process that occurs in children on their way from childhood innocence to adulthood. Too often to notice, we fill our children with dull series of useless facts. I wonder how the future would look if they were encouraged to find (to recall) and not to forget who they really are, which is definitely much more than mere academic accomplishment!

What would happen if, instead of fear of the unknown, we went on to encourage true faith?

. . .

Frane is different. He has always been quiet, somewhat reserved and withdrawn, and he listens more than he ever discusses. He is now a twenty-four-year-old and can no longer be considered a child. There comes a time in the life of every parent when we have to accept that the child has grown up and let him go. As parents, we often make mistakes under the excuse of love, and instead of letting them go and respecting their choices, we offer them our opinions as better and smarter solutions for their lives.

It's hard to let the children go, which is, to a great extent, too delayed in Croatia, but it is definitely individual and dependent on the children's readiness as well. However, I know that it is essential. If we respect children from an early age and believe in them then, when the time comes, we can let them go without fear. However, it requires understanding and accepting that they may not be what we expect of them. They may not become prominent doctors or lawyers and may possibly go in a direction that we would not desire for them. Still, we must respect their choices. Finally, if we let them free, they are less prone to abuse that freedom than they would be when squeezed and imposed upon, trapped in something they try to understand, like, or accept.

I always see parts of me in my children, like the changing image of myself. They often mimic us, and if we look carefully, we will see in them a glimpse of what we love about ourselves and what we'd like to overlook too. Interestingly enough, however, one does not achieve the desired results by trying to change others. It's the same with children. They reflect what we are. We can only change ourselves, and by doing so, we impose changes on our children too.

Life is a dance where we practice and learn by doing small daily steps. Perfection is the totality, not the goal. Being a role model is knowing how to dance with life, when to listen, turn around, and stop. We're best as role models if we are able to live fully, if we are able to loosen up, move on, forgive, and rejoice. Children do not learn by listening to us. Children learn by example—by observing us, by feeling and absorbing.

"How beautiful the two of you are," Mario commented one day with a smile. Sead, my husband and Sara's father, glanced at me. We looked at each other and then back at him, and he explained, "The two of you are beautiful together."

I thought about our nice "dance" together through the last ten years of our life. And it's true. It has been pleasant, and it made me happy to acknowledge it. And that is an example for the children—even if we had made mistakes before or even more because of it.

There is no perfect *one*. Perfection is a whole. Like pieces of a puzzle, we all equally contribute to form a perfect puzzle called the universe. Seemingly apart, still we all dance together to structure the rhythm of life.

Humor,
the Funny Side of Life

I have learned in the past and still go on to discover about the advantages of honest laughter again and again from my own children. I know that this was not always the case. I was not always serious and unable to see the humor in life. I remember that I laughed so much as a child that I was often scolded: "Your eyes laugh all the time! You will get wrinkles from that!" Yet, with years gone by, my sincere smile and the joy from which it was derived, camouflaged in a polite manner and manicured culture with others. I smiled out of habit and never thought it to be offensive to someone. My years in the States had definitely left a mark on my outward behavior, for people in Croatia do not smile as much.

When I started seeing Sead, a few years after my divorce, even though he was plenty polite and often very humorous, he seriously commented several times, "Why do you laugh so much?" I was offended because, accustomed to the fact that I was used to treating all people with politeness and courtesy, I never thought that my smile offered anything else. However, I thought a lot about the comment, and I had to admit to myself that I didn't always feel the sincere joy that should accompany a polite smile. On a number of occasions, I can truly recall, my children subtly tried to awaken the joy in me. I worked a lot, and it somehow seemed unreasonable at the time to look at the funny side of life. On the contrary, I sometimes felt stunned by it. And yet, I smiled politely to others, so as not to show my true feelings, as if they were something shameful or forbidden. I had hidden well from others but also from myself.

One day, while Frane was still in primary school, he brought home a tape of the comedy program, *Mr. Bean,* and gave it to me, saying, "This is for you, Mom. I want to hear you laugh." Although I was a little sick of it, I could not ignore the fact that my son indicated how I lacked genuine humor. Out of a desire to please him, I agreed to give *Mr. Bean* a try, but I expected absolutely nothing. I remember later how we laughed at the nonsense of *Mr. Bean* and watched the tape over and over again. The experience was more than enlightening. I realized that I had become far too stern and that in the race for survival, I forgot the simple, effective things—including the relief of laughter. Since then, I had consciously put effort into finding humor where I had not seen it before. The process still lasts, but it's worthwhile.

Mario, my younger son, had always smiled heartedly from every pore of his body, sincerely and with unadulterated joy. He found humor everywhere, and he spread it to others. When he began to tell jokes, too often I did not see anything funny about them. I often laughed at the fact that he had an almost passionate desire to make others laugh. As he grew, the humor became more subtle, but the joy that flowed from him had remained the same. "Ah, Mom, come, let me give you a hug," he still announces with the same enthusiasm when he appears at the door. His approach taught me that it is possible to laugh at joy that is not a *consequence,* but rather a *cause.*

Over the years, I realized that the power to make others laugh was an art form. Not everyone can make others laugh. It literally relaxes and heals both the giver and the recipient, but sometimes it is necessary to work at it. I don't mean to imply that we should laugh or misleadingly find humor where we do not see it, but still, others cannot make us laugh or smile if we ourselves don't have the capacity or the willingness for it.

Today, my children sometimes—apparently surprised by my progress—say, "What's happening to you, Mom? You're funny!" And it pleases me when I manage to make them laugh and give them back what they have given me—an honest smile on my face.

It's hard to remain unsympathetic of children's laughter, because it is so open, so honest, and so full of joy. They do not need comedy to laugh; they giggle and laugh at small things every day, with such dedication that it is contagious to listen. And those who avoid their laughter and look down on their smile are exactly the ones who need to find it most within themselves.

"I smile to joy!"

—Cvita (age 5)

To Dream and to Desire

For years, I was frustrated because I did not know exactly what to wish for in life. Somehow it was easier to define what I *didn't* want.

Inspired by the proclamation of a fancy—the dream is everything—I felt myself drawn into it by my own lack of awareness. In search of "something that is uniquely mine," I had repeatedly tried to force an outline of a supposedly strong dream on various pieces of paper. It seemed to be important at the time to write it down on paper for it to come true. I was afraid not to write anything. When I was told to write a date by each dream, I did that too. I followed instructions to the smallest detail, but still these dreams of mine did not come true.

"Why?" I had asked myself repeatedly, but then it dawned on me.

My dreams were not dreams; they were desperate hopes of salvation out of some unbearable situations. I did not accept being where I was: there and then. I chose not to deal with the reality at hand; I chose to be present in the future.

It was only recently that I realized I was on to something that could have a broader meaning for me. When, instead of a date-determined dream, I began to feel something of a fervent desire, things began to change. It was not difficult to determine the direction to follow. I just needed to follow my instincts—the voice and the feeling within that supported my vision. I realized that what had bothered me the most in the past was being locked on determining the future. What might have brought security to some imposed on me as something pre-ordained and too forced and uninspired. It was the mistrust in anything that was not planned and dwelled upon with which I finally disagreed. Not that I enjoy unpleasant surprises in life, but I realized that life is far too interesting to be frantically planned about. In a desire to achieve, we just might miss an aspiration that is woven into every dream—the magic of creation—which is much greater than our own imagination. We forget to live and enjoy life. We totally forget who we are.

Maybe the secret is to find out which supposed dreams to follow and which to disregard. Some of my dreams have not come true, even if I had written them down on paper and dwelled upon them. But back then, I did not have the ability to distinguish dreams of the mind and ego from those of the heart, and probably I was a bit afraid to. Dreams of the ego dwell upon success, which can be measured by means of wealth or status, whereas dreams of the heart dwell upon the satisfaction within. It is much easier to picture ourselves as obtaining what is preordained by the mind than what is of the heart. To follow the heart might mean being teased and misunderstood, because the heart chooses irrationally without planning. But what we fail to foresee is the true reward of such a pursuit. When we discern desires of ego and those of the heart, the rewards come daily in the form of living in the magic of now, and that is beyond what we can ever plan. I believe that we are rewarded in life by life itself when we follow our true hearts' desires. Just because we cannot always see the target doesn't mean that we are not going in the right direction. I do not need to know everything to still believe that there is much of everything in store for me.

Looking far into the goal, I was unable to enjoy the process of being me. I was a brand-new Vesna after years of working on myself, but still I lacked the confidence in life, the faith that comes only from within. Maybe I did live for a while as a control freak, trying to predict the smallest details of the future. But I found out that it doesn't work well that way. What an irony! I learned that everything takes place more easily and with a more desirable outcome when you give up frantic control. When you have a desire, recognize it, act upon it, and believe, but do not dwell upon it and massacre it with pre-ordained determination and daily repetitions of a dreamlike fixation. That is a sure way to kill a dream.

I had often found myself under the influence of what others suggested to me—fight stronger, be more, crave more, do more, be more willing to sacrifice yourself, feel less and think.

I was really troubled. I had changed so many things in the last years, and I believed that I had done well for myself, but then it was implied once again that I should change that which was so hard to obtain. This constant insufficiency caused me terrible frustrations. For an instant, I know now, because my own doubt surfaced again, and my ego once again took control, I had disregarded all that I believed in and worked on, just to indulge into a fantasy of an instant dream come true. One day, unexpectedly, it hit me again. I remembered! I need not be someone else. I know who I am. I need not be a part of someone else's dream. I need only be me, accept me—because my way, the way I do things, despite imperfections, is unique: live life in the now unburdened, be honest, free, at peace with myself, listen and follow the voice from my heart. That is my destiny, the essence and the purpose of my life.

To follow one's own heart, one's own destiny, is to desire growth and development, rather than attempt to control what cannot be controlled.

Now I know I did not listen to my own words sometimes: "It doesn't feel right!" I would hear myself argue over and over again, only to dismiss my own feelings. For a long time, this subtle voice of my intuition fought to surface for recognition, but what was imposed by society and environment often dominated. I sought myself outside my own boundaries in external things that did not satisfy my needs. Out of fear that I might be ridiculed, because I was "soft," and because I listened to my heart, many times I found myself in situations where I satisfied someone else's dreams and desires and not mine. And each time, I had repeatedly found myself in an insignificant fight, disappointed with the outcome. Yet, here I am.

It might again seem as if I had just made another sudden decision, but once more I know the truth: this is something that has been smoldering in me for a long time, waiting for recognition. This is my heart's desire. This is my role in this life. My name is Vesna, and like the meaning of my name—the Goddess of Spring—I stand for change and growth. I learn and grow and teach. I am a teacher at heart. I follow my heart, even when I do not know exactly what tomorrow brings. I live in faith and feel peace. I notice the birds at dawn and listen to the rain. I watch the sun come up in the morning and feel how its rays touch my face. I feel my body, and I listen to its messages. I heal from the inside out. I mute thoughts and listen. I have no specific plans, yet an incredible number of new possibilities arise daily. I do what I love and love what I do. No senseless action needs to be done in order to prepare for the moment in the future. For the first time, I resist the very thing that I have been taught throughout life and abandon it—the need to control. Still, I do not allow the current to carry me along unwillingly. I travel from coast to coast without stopping for long, and I listen. There are no expectations. I feel quiet joy, and I do not have the need to scream to be heard. I have nothing to prove. I am stepping out into the unknown terrain, but I am no longer afraid. I feel as if all my life so far has been just groundwork for what's about to come. I have no more need to follow; I have learned. This is my path, and I truly enjoy the process. I still stumble sometimes and make undesirable turns, but now I know how to get back on track.

My dream is not to dream but to wake up in a desire for the fullness of life and the peace within; to avoid the harsh discipline of planning in the future tense; to achieve every day; to stand tentative in action; not to limit—to allow change, growth, and progress to happen naturally.

There is a catch, though. It comes in the form of the meaning of a little word called *faith*. Indeed, we are only limited by the boundaries of our faith. We are afraid of the unknown, when we should actually fear the well-known. We live in a world of cause and consequences of ego, inspired by what is and what has happened around us, but we ignore what lies within. We allow competition, and we struggle to be accepted as normal, but it need not be, unless we *believe* that it must. And even that is just a step we must undertake to learn and grow. Perhaps it's not, "I think—therefore I am," but it is definitely true that "Whatever I think—I am."

With tremendous effort for a better life, we forget the simplest, most fundamental possibility—to stop, listen, and wait. At a time when we charge ourselves with a beating rate to align with the prospective universal rhythm, in fear that we might miss out on something, I often hear the anxious words: "I have no time!" But who determines time? Each one of us for ourselves. To have or not to have time is the mind's own perception, and from my own life experience, I know that the amount of time we have is a matter of our own choice, but to make the necessary purge is up to us.

How many things do we do, needlessly wasting precious time?

To how many activities do we have to take our kids a week to satisfy our ego and meet with the expectations of others?

Life is not a fight. Life is not a race. This is just a marketing trick of modern times that offers existence in the form of endless possibilities of nothingness.

Do we really need all these things that are presented to us?

Just a peek into our homes will determine how many bits and pieces we buy and do not use. We accumulate endlessly. We buy toys for our children to play with, to replace our playing with the children.

When did simplicity lose its charm?

Buried—in our minds, homes, and the bustle around us—we cannot find peace. To find it, we need to stop and remember once again who we are. We are much more than it appears at first, but constant distractions remind us otherwise.

"I wish that my wishes would come true!"

—Sara's New Year's wish (age 6)

The Successes and the Failures

It seems as if people occupy their minds with the same things over and over again:

"Did you succeed?"

"Will you succeed?"

We use the word *success* every day, when referring to all the little obstacles that we overcome on a daily basis but also when it comes to sizing up something that is considered a totality of life. Many books cover the topic of success, but very few determine what they mean by it.

What is success?

I believe that success should be treated as something personal, as *a level of one's own personal growth*. Still, success is quite predetermined as of yet and offered in terms of attainment—the amount of accumulated money and wealth and that of reaching a desired goal.

Success as an Achievement of Goals . . .

I stand witness to the fact that many people and organizations, some which I have encountered, see success almost exclusively as an achievement of goals. Therefore, it seems a logical imperative to be able to identify a goal. I always saw the goal as something fixed in the future, a point in time that helps us establish the direction of our movement and eases the making of everyday choices. *If you know exactly where to go,* I thought, *you can easily make decisions along the way.* Because of the desired outcome, an aberration was not an option, for it would have meant a loss of focus with respect to the target. But staying on track proved to be most challenging for me, because it bypassed the magic of the unknown and the creativity that I enjoy the most.

What's in a goal?

For athletes, the goal is the finish line in the Olympic Games, the gold medal, and the obstacle is to find the quickest way to it. So, even if the goal is reachable within one hundred yards, the trip can last for years.

Why?

In sports, as much as we sometimes stress the importance of the journey, we actually only remember the winners, the ones who have reached the goal first, the ones who were a fragment of a second faster than their predecessors, the medalists. It's quite easy to image the frustration of those who do not win a medal, because the winners are few and there is always only one first place; only one is the fastest and the best.

Can one justify years of work, effort, and toil, struggle and failure in the end?

Maybe life is a struggle and it is not fair. Maybe things are tough in life, and maybe we sometimes succeed and sometimes we don't.

But if we do not succeed, does that mean we are a failure?

Failure is often defined as the opposite of success. Even though failure today takes on other attributes, it still remains a struggle and a frustration when you constantly try really hard and do not achieve expectedly. You must not give up! Never! This is what I hear very often, and instead of inspiring me, it has bothered me a lot in the past.

How many years of failure can a person endure in order to be able to give up with dignity?

Where is the limit?

When can we take into account that a certain goal is simply unattainable for a particular person?

Can we accept what we call failure equally to what we call success?

> *"If at first you don't succeed, try, try again. Then quit.*
> *There's no point in being a damn fool about it."*

> **—W.C. Fields**

It might not even be that the person is not good enough to achieve a certain goal; I believe that it is often just not the right path for the person to follow, and thus the goal is unachievable.

Giving up is an unpopular decision, because our culture is unkind to those who give up or stray from the goal. "Until death, but to not give up," is the motto of many. And it might give some a perspective and a meaning in life, but for someone like me, I'm certain that it will not. Many fight because giving up is an unpopular option. Books and billboards say: *Winners have it all. Winners do not quit.*

Giving up should not always be considered a sign of weakness but a sign of mere prudence. Maybe the lesson to learn is not that of winning. Giving up something that constantly eludes your reach may offer you the possibility of success in another field. Someone may not be the best athlete, but maybe he's a great coach. Perhaps professional sports is entirely not his desired field of work, but the idea of enjoying it in his free time with no pressure to achieve is. Perhaps the fight on the outside is not worthy because it is the struggle within a man that prepossesses.

Why do we achieve?

Is it for the sake of others or for us?

Whom are we afraid of disappointing?

I do not believe that failure is in opposition to success. Even though success is sweet, we learn from failure just as much or even more. If success brings happiness, and I've mentioned earlier that we do not learn a great deal from happiness, how then can the lack of success be considered a failure?

With so many participants in life and only a few winners, there are only so many success stories! The winner is not necessarily the one who has worked the hardest but maybe the one who has just followed his heart's desire, his talents, and his own path; he succeeded because the set goal was something that had personally fulfilled him, and he did not work; rather, he played, and the struggle was not a struggle but a pleasure of the heart. Crossing the finish line was natural fulfillment of his own purpose. For many others, it is simply not so. It is not their hundred miles to go. The finish line is not their destiny. For them, continued work in the same field is sacrifice and a constant fight and a struggle of the mind, until they realize otherwise—until they learn. Maybe they are not considered winners, as we know that the winners are few in every competition. But maybe we should not impose upon ourselves to defeat others but rather to conquer ourselves, so that we win our own inner battles and predicaments and find the peace within. Maybe others will not know or care to notice, but we will. We'll know the difference.

> *"The man who has done his level best . . . is a success, even though the world may write him down a failure."*

> **—B. C. Forbes**

The competition itself imposes loss and failure. Yet, constantly, as if we enjoy this torture, from the earliest age, we encourage competitive spirit in preschool and elementary schools, in high schools and colleges, at work, and in all walks of life. Be honest—who likes to lose?

But then, how many times in life are we first?

The world would be a sad place if we were to concentrate only on acceptable successes in life. There wouldn't even be winners if there was no place for "losers." Perhaps the only real purpose of the ones who lose is to make the winners look good and to push the boundaries for the next competition. Maybe it is just like everything else: we need both experiences in life, but loss is more common because there is a lot to be learned from it. I don't know for sure, but I conclude from my own findings in life. I used to be very competitive too, and I had instructed others to be that way. Today, I prefer not to compete with others but rather to see through my own little battles, seek my path, and follow it open-heartedly, because we never know what unexpected blessings life has in store for us.

Success as an Achievement of Wealth, Fame, or Social Status . . .

The word *wealth* is very commonly misused as meaning exclusively material wealth—property or money, but it can also define the richness of the spirit, which is often not reflected in the material but as an internal state of mind of each person. One does not exclude the other, even though we often witness that the two are opposites from which we judge with exclusivity. Sometimes a considerably rich person will look down on those who have less as, on the other hand, will a person dedicated only to spiritual development look down upon those who amass. More often than not, we witness that both sides have gone off course. It has always been easy to judge, but I see no need for condemnation, regardless of the position. Attaining both spiritual and material wealth at the same time seems natural if we follow our life's purpose, but still, all other options are just as open and imposing. I see no reason why an internally prosperous individual cannot be materially rewarded as well. It is also not sensible to think that people with large amounts of money and property cannot be spiritual. I believe we are generously rewarded for our creativity, and each one of us is granted a seed of growth, but it's up to us to discover the specific kind. Each one of us is special, even if we do not see it. The discovery of this special seed in oneself opens the path to abundance both material and spiritual. Is it not natural that we are rewarded for what arises exclusively from our inherent attributes and abilities and our God-given talents? These are our gifts to humanity, progress and evolution of mankind, and the prize for the discovery and creative expression of will, the success which comes easy, without struggle and despair.

> *"Don't aim for success if you want it; just do what you love and believe in, and it will come naturally."*
>
> *—David Frost*

We've all heard about "the price of glory," which is a frequent companion to someone who has achieved a general familiarity or public attention. It either attracts or petrifies us. Fame implies a loss of anonymity. There is no glory without disclosure. And while some will do anything just to come under the spotlight, others abhor the thought that they might be overwhelmed by attention. Amusingly enough, we all play roles in life, and here begins the one between the observer and the observed, the ones in the shadow and the ones exposed. Ones without the others do not exist, as cantankerous as it may become sometimes, throwing dust into the eyes of the other. Achieving fame in the public eye often becomes the cause for envy; we tend to forget what let a person rise on the pedestal of fame, and in time we notice only the trivialities compared to talents. Eventually the performers themselves often forget their primary purpose and engage in playing a diverse role. What happens?

The roles we play and our purpose in life may vary a lot. We often forget who we are, or we are still in the search for it. The role is the part we choose to play in the drama we call *life*. The purpose is the deeper meaning and the point of life. Once again, we need to return to the ingenuity that comes from within us and find our purpose in existence. And although we cannot avoid playing these roles in life—a mother, a daughter, a father, a son, a teacher, a doctor, or a judge—it is good to notice and ask ourselves:

What lies beneath?

We tend to equate success with the position that a person enjoys at work and in society. I'm sure it can be justified because one can really feel rewarded because of the position acquired. Nevertheless, it is a role one person plays. Fame, superficially speaking, can be labeled as success, but it does not guarantee happiness.

Shouldn't personal happiness be the first factor of success?

Happiness should not be regarded as that of one's spouse, children, parents, relatives, or friends, but rather of our own unconditional content.

Is personal happiness selfish?

I don't believe it to be true. A person who hasn't reached a personal level of satisfaction can almost never be happy for others or make others happy. Setting goals and achieving the so-called successes can be inspiring but only if it leads to inner satisfaction and peace—if it is not just a point in the future but rather a daily step, the journey and not the target.

What is success if it doesn't make you happy? What benefit am I to my husband if I am miserable? What kind of a role model can I be for my children if I do not enjoy life? Can a parent be content watching his child's misfortune? Who likes to listen to his or her relatives moan about their inevitable fate? How long can our friends endure our sorrow until they themselves are drawn into it? What use are we to our employer if we, because of dissatisfaction, constantly make mistakes? What contribution do we make to society if we allow ourselves to rely on welfare? What is our contribution to the evolution of humanity if we do not create?

Personal happiness and inner peace are an imperative, and they follow a heart's desire.

I didn't get it for a long time. I always thought that I had to make others happy, but the truth is that I can only make *myself* happy, and by doing so, others around me will feel the vibrations too. Happiness is contagious.

If I do not feel joy in life, I cannot create and contribute. My goal is inner peace and faith that it can be acquired on a daily basis. It has no date in the future. It is in the now. When I feel joy, I'm sure, everyone around me feels it too. Happiness, however, requires the absence of expectations, jealousy, and bluster. It doesn't struggle to prove anything. It simply is.

Success is taking small steps every day to better ourselves. It is finding out who we are. It is finding joy and inner peace on a daily basis. Success is finding out what we want to do in life, finding the one thing or many things that make us happy and then committing to it respectfully. Success is embracing the idea that not all can be carefully planned out and letting go of controls, so that the magic of life can work for us. Success is embracing the idea that the happiness of one person will have an impact on the happiness of others as well. Happiness is something we share by touching the souls of others mildly, easily, and joyfully.

Success is manifested in the faith of its carrier.

> *"Success is blocked by concentrating on it and planning for it . . .*
>
> *Success is shy—it won't come out while you're watching."*

—*Tennessee Williams*

About Religion and Belief

It has always amazed me how some people so certainly declare: "I am not a believer!" What do they mean? Is it even possible not to believe?

"But you don't go to church; I didn't think you were a believer!"

"Oh, but I am," I had explained for the umpteenth time without really wanting to get into a deeper discussion.

The time has finally come to clarify some points.

I was born into a traditional Catholic family and raised with a spirit of respect for the elderly and the fear of God. Decisions made in early childhood were directly connected to Him. If we were not allowed to do something, it was because of our very strict mom, the elderly in the house, or God. Mom did not see everything, but God did; so we were told. It would be an understatement to say that I was just afraid. Images of Jesus and saints hung all over the walls of our house, and they pointed with threatening fingers, "I see you," which reinforced fear to my immature mind. I felt their eyes on me, even when I didn't look. I did not want to infringe upon their laws, but at one point, I remember that I had gathered just enough courage to take down a picture off our bedroom wall, one that had been hanging there for as long as I could remember. I hid it under the bed and naively thought that no one would notice. *There,* I thought, *now you can't see.* That was true only until Mom noticed the lack of the effigy and returned it to its place.

"You've got to be good and obey," she warned me, because even though I was mostly obedient, I was also the liveliest and most mischievous one.

Mom and Dad were the epitome of good in our house. As far as I can remember, they tried hard to live by God's law. We felt their connection and love, and their behavior hid no surprises. They're as predictable today as they were then.

Subjected to the same incentives, situations, the same people, and the same environment, we cannot expect a lot of change to occur—a major shift in personal growth and development, thinking, or behavior. Even at an early age, I was often in contact with different people and situations. I was the one who moved around a lot, but to my understanding of religion, it was life in America that had contributed the most. Another environment, completely different people, diverse relationships, another point of view, books—it all added up to form a different opinion on life, religion, and belief.

I've noticed that a lot of things change in your mind when you shift your viewpoint. It's like losing balance. You have to do everything to restore it, but it doesn't mean that you won't fall in the process. Regaining balance means shifting, and getting up doesn't mean that you will end up in the same spot. You might even change your position purposely. The fall enabled you to see from another perspective and learn.

In the States, contrary to life back home, I discovered the flexibility of the concept of religion. I discovered that religion and belief are connected but in reality vary a lot. To my surprise, I found out that I could avoid Sunday Mass if my aunt sent an envelope with my name and some money inside. That was convenient, and it made me feel as if the American God was less fearful than my mom's. I loosened up. Eventually, by the time I was thirteen, I stopped going to church, with the exception of Christmas and Easter. My critical mind found objections even in the smallest rituals of worship. I was overly critical and too rigid for the years that I wore. To me, all religions that I'd encountered then qualified as vague and limiting. I felt that many, including myself, came to church out of habit and/or fear. As I saw it, Mass was a regular massive sin-redemption ceremony. I watched people around me sin and pray simultaneously, even though the preaching of tolerance, faith, love, and charity were clearly worshiped, but still jealousy, greed, selfishness, judgment, resentment, criticism, and control were a big part of it too. I began to notice that religion alone did not make people any better or any happier.

> *"I like your Christ; I do not like your Christians.*
> *Your Christians are so unlike your Christ."*
>
> **—Mahatma Gandhi**

When I came back to Croatia, I chose to conform to the rigid routines of my family's worship, not so much because I felt the need for it again but because it was expected of me and I didn't want to disappoint again. It took a lot of years for me to set my beliefs straight and to take a stand once again. For ten years, I stayed in a marriage that just didn't work out, for fear of condemnation, sin, and God's revenge, because there were constant reminders that hell existed as well as heaven. Heaven awaited the good, and hell was for the disobedient. It seemed obvious which side I was on.

With time passing, it seemed as if my choices narrowed down to hell, no matter what I chose to accomplish; the chance for flaw and condemnation was guaranteed. Between two nightmares, I finally chose the one that seemed more acceptable.

In the turmoil of divorce, still there were many factors that worked to my advantage. The fact that I had moved away from my immediate family, away from the island and into the city, away from being watched over and controlled, consequently freed me, and I was able to think, feel, and mold without apparent distractions. Only then did I enjoy going to Sunday Mass at noon, the Mass for young people and children—not to pray but rather to feel and to mend. With ten-year-old Frane by my side and unborn Mario curled up in my stomach, I felt safe and peaceful. It relaxed me and brought tranquility to the rest of the week. If ever I enjoyed any church rituals, it was then. I felt no resentment, no condemnation or criticism. I felt unburdened by the melodies that had linked all of those young souls in a song. The words were not as important as the vibrations that filled the church and my soul as well. Strangely enough, as I felt more and more content, due to my regained self-respect, with time my need for Sunday ceremonies slowly faded away. At a time when there was no peace to be found within myself, I was thankful even for the feeling that was offered through Sunday Mass. But it soon became clear enough—I needed to find peace that would not fade away with Sundays.

At a critical point in my life when I believed, "if it doesn't kill me, it will strengthen me," as I was struggling to meet the harsh existence and the even more difficult burden of divorce, I found comfort in my children and the books that I read. Slowly but surely, faith emerged and transcended the narrow boundaries of a religion, only to become a belief in myself.

I remember how I reacted to a book that was given to me by a cousin at the time. The book spoke of a God who punishes. Even though it made me furious, it made me think too. I was mad at my cousin, because as far I as was concerned, he gave me the book only to point out how I would be punished by God for my sins. After all, it was he who once said, "We are all blacksmiths of our own happiness." I felt as if the book was a direct attack upon my decision to persist on change in my life. I know now that there's more to it. I know that the whole incident was somehow just a mirror image of my still-weakened beliefs. I remember the anger that I felt then and how I said no once and for all to God who judges, God who criticizes and punishes. *If we are God's creations,* I thought, *God should be love.*

I knew that I had come to a breaking point, a point of no return, when I realized that it was not God but I who had to forgive and forget. It took a lot time and work to straighten my beliefs, but I still feel the benefits of that decision now, fifteen years later. I don't go to church anymore, because I don't feel the need for it, but I don't forbid my children to go if they wish to. My experience with religion taught me that we must find belief within ourselves first. Of course, the road to awareness is not always paved. Our children have their paths to follow and their lessons to learn. Will they make mistakes? Of course; so have we.

Today I feel free because I know that there is nothing out there that doesn't lie inside of me too. Whenever I feel distressed, I ask myself the question: "What should I do?" If I am patient enough and ready to hear, the answer always comes—not in the form one might expect, but it always comes, if I believe that it will come. So, I am not religious but I have a lot of faith, more faith than many I know. My belief lies inside of me, and it cannot be taken away by anyone but me. I believe in the miracle of life.

> *"You cannot believe in God until you believe in yourself."*
>
> **—Swami Vivekananda**

Marriage and Belief

It's very easy to judge why many marriages today end in divorce, but we should not. Just like parents do their best, given the level of consciousness at the time, so do married couples. It only seems that the number of divorces nowadays is higher. Formally, it may be, but in reality, I believe that many would have ended their marriages in the past too, had that been socially acceptable. I remember what my old aunt said once about her marriage to the man who had harmed me as a child: "I would have divorced him, but that was not popular to do when I was young." She stayed for the ride, as many did. A few years later, she died an alcoholic, despaired and disillusioned. Her husband lived for many years later.

We may not always understand why things happen the way they do but I am sure there is a greater reason for it, and somehow the choices are always ours to make.

Marriage is not about whether we can endure or not. It is all about whether we know who we are or not. Divorce happens because we try to find in others the qualities that we cannot find in ourselves—love, compassion, kindness, forgiveness, strength, humor. When our partner changes, we complain and again look for faults so much that we cannot see the ones in ourselves. The fact of the matter is, those who have found the peace within will easily be able to live in peace with others. Those who are at peace with themselves will find some of the same qualities in their partners.

When Sead came into my life a few years after my divorce, I was a different person. There was little that remained of the Vesna before. I was stronger but gentler yet, more tolerant, and confident enough that I was on the right track. Still, even if I my family no longer hassled me about my beliefs, I knew what was bothering them about Sead—his origin. Some said it out loud, and some had it written across their faces.

"Is he Catholic?" they wondered. "Does he go to church?"

Although I was not bothered by what others thought, even if they were my family, I knew that religion, not faith, could largely complicate coexistence. I did not mind when he said that he was an atheist; he explained that he did not believe in God or anything else. It made me laugh inside, because I felt that few people can really have no faith at all. Even though his father's roots were Islamic, we both agreed that organized religion did not correspond with either. For me, an act of birth is already a miracle and a reflection of faith, but freedom of each individual is to be or not be linked to religion, any organized system of belief and worship.

Our life together is blessed in faith, not that of a religion but that of faith in love, life, and the sense that we are all connected, even if declared otherwise by religions. I am not surprised that many people would still believe what had been declared by writing, verified by man, and organized, rather than what arises from such seemingly imperfect origin as we see ourselves to be.

Can we take responsibility?

Can we embrace our insecurities instead of replacing them with others?

Would life be simpler if we did not have to think about belonging to this religion or that religion?

Can we believe in life in the coexistence of differences as our means of learning a lesson?

Can we learn to live in love, tolerance, and peace?

If religion ceased to exist, would there be more faith?

> *"There is no need for temples, no need for complicated philosophies. My brain and my heart are my temples; my philosophy is kindness."*
>
> **—Dalai Lama**

PART THREE

The Path of the Heart

"A free man is led by his heart. There is no knowledge that is beyond him. He carries the entire universe and everything available to him from within. He is the creator of his reality and his destiny. He takes responsibility. The pupil becomes the teacher.

—Adrian Predrag Kezele

A few months ago, I had a desire. I decided to follow it and dared take a step into the unknown. Led by a decision of the heart, I decided to write a book—nothing particularly new or revolutionary, just an act of fulfilling my own desires to better understand the whys of my life. Even though I have thought about writing a book in the past, it was for all the wrong reasons. Long ago, I wanted to hurt those who had hurt me. But that was a long time ago, and I have changed a lot since then. My reasons for writing this book fulfill another purpose. Even if I lacked the audacity, the courage, and the confidence for it, I needed to do it, and it wasn't until I was almost finished that I understood the reasons behind it. We don't always understand everything that we do, and we don't need to, but we do need to follow our heart.

Writing in the quiet of my home in the early mornings, I was able to take a look at my life from a different perspective. Describing some events for the first time in my life, I was able to write about them without the feelings that have always impeded me before. I was able to understand the hidden meanings of some events, and I went on to share some of the findings with Sead, my sister Maria, and my friends, without resentment. I was ready to heal.

The obstacle that I had to overcome was the neglect of faith at a time when my world shouted: "There is no time!" The excessive labeling of "winner or loser" attitude of many and the need to control even that what we believe—"choose something and believe in it" drives us right into the arms of our ego and further away from what we really are. In the midst of a promise of achieving a financial breakthrough, I had decided to do what I feared the most—give up on a set goal, step aside, and believe that my heart knows what is best for me.

This is a personal story, an opinion, in abundance of stories and personal truths, yet the real truth is located in the hearts of each one of us, and it is only a matter of time before we reach inside and begin to unravel the wonders that are concealed there. In a situation where we do not see the light of day, it is difficult to blindly believe that something happens for our own good. We tend to favor the possession of things and the bearing of flattering titles to set us free, but the illusion is obvious once achieved in the absence of the heart. We can seemingly have the whole lot and still have nothing at all. The things around us are mere shallow condolences if we don't have a full heart. To obtain the fullness of the heart is always to reach inside.

It is then easy to understand how suffering is a teacher in the way of knowledge; happiness, though enticing, teaches little if anything at all; good fortune is appreciated only after the hardship we've experienced before.

Today I can say I'm grateful that I had the opportunity to learn the lessons that have enriched my life. Not that I would have chosen them deliberately, but from this perspective, it is not difficult to forgive and understand the necessity of such a past. However, it has taken years and years of work on the sheer identification of its purpose. But I feel free and relieved and no longer ask, "Why did it have to happen to me?" Now I'm just thankful that I have been able to recognize its meaning and heal. For that matter, I am grateful for everyone I have encountered along the way. I am grateful for the lessons. Life is no longer something that saddens me. I look forward to little things I did not notice before. Unburdened by expectations, I give my best. I give and I receive abundantly.

Everything lies within. We just need to reach deep enough to reveal who we are: the flaws we need to change, people we need to forgive, and the meanings we need to look for. The mere desire is not enough. We have to work. Desires are a gift, but it's up to us how we act. We do not get the final solutions in life, but just an incentive, a preference, or a gift, and then we take those steps that naturally impose as a way to fulfill the desires. We will discover that the way to fulfillment carries in itself a variety of obstacles and messages, but only if we are open and willing to learn will we enjoy the process, which is more important than the goal itself.

Sometimes we dig up something we do not desire, something we resist. But what we resist the most is just the thing to perceive. If we do not accept it as a message to learn and grow, life will yet again thrust another lesson our way, and only by stopping and recognizing it can we see the greater purpose and overcome it. We go on when we are ready to learn.

I do not pretend to understand all the mysteries of life or all the ways of the soul, but I do know one thing: resistance is futile. And just when we think we have no other choice, we have just that—another option—to accept or not to accept a situation where we are now. Changing the perspective often changes what we see. Sometimes we just do not look deep enough, or we do not see the wider context. We are not alone in this world. To live in harmony with everything around us is our destiny. Sometimes others are in the service of our maturity, but sometimes we are a part of the broader picture and help someone else mature. A shift to another position points out things more concretely than running away from situations that we do not understand.

I find that everything has a purpose, and that spurred my healing process, as did the people and situations around me. We are not alone. We just seem like lonely islands, but we are linked in the depths we anticipate to notice. But there is a connection.

Our parents, siblings, children, friends, and acquaintances are not just that. They are all our teachers in the way of life, each with its own purpose of existence and each with a higher purpose of touching the soul with which they dance the cosmic dance. How easily we dismiss life, but how stunning and perfect that dance is, that which is imposed on a daily basis to keep in a sequence that can be perceived. Because there is no happiness without sadness or feeling that we live without knowing that we are expendable and mortal. To live through it all is the purpose of the soul, which has more than enough time to spare.

If we realize that life has a purpose of learning and enlightenment and the evolution of mankind, can we then accept and embrace what we do not quite understand? Can we recognize and become aware that what lies behind each obstacle has its own beauty and is for the good of all, for prosperity and progress? What are our options otherwise? We continue to fight against everything—deny, reject, criticize, and defy all powers and almost everything in ourselves. Only after years, perhaps decades or more living in the struggle, maybe we understand: when we stop resisting, all barriers drop, and solutions miraculously appear. They have been there before, patiently waiting for our indulgence, undisturbed by time passing.

Should we complain? How much is enough? Enough is when we recognize it—the moment of illumination, the revelation itself. Our soul is not in a hurry. In addition, no one can manage us as efficiently as we can. No one else can act upon us as strongly as we do. At the core of every problem lies a solution and the choice—whether to come to grips with ourselves or to ignore it.

We should not judge. Accepting that we are disciples in the way of life on Earth, we should forgive ourselves the need to criticize others, because we are all students. Some are only in preschool, some in elementary school, some have graduated, and some have gotten their PhDs in life. Do not misinterpret, though. A school diploma is not always a witness to the individual's level of consciousness. A seemingly ordinary person we may have overlooked may carry a message for us and may be at a higher level of consciousness than someone pursuing a seemingly successful career.

Everyone has his or her own path to follow. Sometimes we share a segment, sometimes we meet at the intersection, but we all live our unique lives. It is always a journey into the unknown, because we do not know exactly what life has in store for us, and we cannot know. We can plan everything in detail, but still we cannot see or predict everything. Recognize that our way is ours alone and that it's unique, as we are unique in the freedom of expression, creation, and life that is creatively ours too. The possibilities are endless. The path we walk is always a journey into the unknown, but it is only a question of whether we embrace or reject it.

It is ours to remember who we are. We should not be afraid to be led by our hearts, and we should not fear the unknown. We should embrace life, because it is our own creation!

By accepting life as a whole, we give ourselves the opportunity to explore the uncharted; we open ourselves to love and the process of change that enriches us. To be true to oneself is a gift and our right, but we should allow others to be themselves too. To enjoy freedom, we must grant it to others first. To feel peace and tranquility and to spread it silently through the hearts of others is our destiny. To know that each one of us is special, to wake up and step out boldly into the unknown, is to accept the magic of life. To support the child within and the curiosity, the joy, and the laughter is a welcoming sign of who we really are. To break free from the fear of darkness is to have faith. Even the darkest night hides dawn at its doorstep.

The miracle of life is happening now in all of us.

The undertaken journey of my life has been well worthwhile. It has been for my own good—for the lessons I had to learn; for greater good; for the fact that I now see beyond the obvious, and I'm thankful for it. For the fact that I no longer ask:

Why did it have to happen to me?

> *"Knowing is not enough; we must apply. Willing is not enough; we must do."*
>
> **—Johann Wolfgang von Goethe**

The Recollection of Thoughts

About Suffering

Suffering inflicts pain because we are afraid. It haunts us because we try to escape from it. To be unwavering, to be unafraid, to love suffering rather than trying to flee from it is to taste its deep, sweet surrender. The resistance is what hurts. Suffering is a just a personal conception of the mind. It's as real as you make it.

If there is a higher purpose for suffering, it is to make us learn and grow.

In order to grow, we must take steps:

1. Forgiveness—We start by forgiving ourselves and then others around us.

2. Responsibility—We take responsibility for our lives. Blaming others doesn't give desired results.

3. Desire to learn—We must be armed with desire to learn in order to take a step forward.

4. Acceptance—Sometimes we even have to accept what seems unacceptable and show faith that everything happens for a greater good.

5. Healing—Healing happens when we surrender from fight, not life itself.

6. Growth—We leap onto the next level of consciousness when we learn a lesson.

About Choices

1. Acceptance or denial—When we accept, we take a step forward. When we are in denial, we take a step backward.

2. Faith or control—We can choose to believe that our desires are gifts and have patience for them to manifest, or we can try to control the universe.

To believe that birth is a choice is to imply:

Choice is the first sign of freedom, the one thing no one can take away from us. Even as children, we make choices that affect our lives. We always have at least two choices to choose from. We always choose to accept or deny. The choices that we make can make us happy or unhappy but they are still choices, nevertheless. There is no wrong choice. Each one teaches a specific lesson.

Good intentions and desires are not enough. It is necessary to act.

Whether we believe that the choices are ours to make or we believe that they are not—either way, we are right.

Being focused on what has happened or what will be deprives us of what we can experience now. It deprives us of the magic of being.

About Friends

Friends are people you can rely on in the hardest of times.

A friend holds your hand while you grow stronger and then thrusts you into the world so you can find the pillar of strength in yourself.

We carry our friends in our hearts, no matter where we are or where they might be.

∞

You don't have to be rich, well-known, highly educated, or look like a star, and yet you can be special to that one person at least, and it makes a big difference in that someone's life. Sometimes even the smallest things matter, and you never know what those might be. And as much as hurt clings to the heart, so does an honest and warm gesture, especially when it comes from those we love.

About Change

There is no guarantee that we will one day awaken in life and begin its transformation. No one can help us if we are cloistered to change. If we believe that there is darkness or that there is light at the end of the corridor, either way, we are right. What we believe shapes our lives. We decide. We choose and we change.

∞

The search for the external does not help us find what lies within.

We find the highest values when we close our eyes and dare to take a look inside.

We are afraid of the unknown when we should actually fear the well-known.

∞

Buried—in our minds, homes, and the bustle around us—we cannot find peace. To find it, we need to stop and remember once again who we are. We are much more than it appears at first, but constant distractions remind us otherwise.

∞

I have learned that it is wise to accept both the good and bad in life. Take the good with gratitude, nourish it with love, and spread it to others. The very thing that bothers you most, that which makes you angry and despaired, accept courageously and embrace, because just like the beautiful things in life, it is a part of you which, if you wish to alter, you must first recognize within. In order to grow, you must be willing to change.

About Success

Success is personal growth.

Success is taking small steps every day to better ourselves. It is finding out who we are. It is finding joy and inner peace on a daily basis. Success is finding out what we want to do in life, finding the one or the many things that make us happy and then committing to it respectfully. Success is embracing the idea that not all can be carefully planned out and letting go of controls so that the magic of life can work for us. Success is embracing the idea that the happiness of one person will have an impact on the happiness of others as well. Happiness is not something we possess. It is something we share by touching the souls of others mildly, easily, and joyfully.

Success is manifested in the faith of its carrier.

I have learned that everything takes place more easily and with a more desirable outcome when you give up frantic control. When you have a desire, recognize it, act upon it, and believe, but do not dwell on it and massacre it with pre-ordained determination and daily repetitions of a dreamlike fixation. That is a sure way to kill a dream.

Special thanks

Special thanks to my mother and father in-law, Vesna and Nazif, who have accepted me as their own and who have always been there for me. I have longed for home for most of my life, only to find that I now have more than one.

Friends come and friends go physically, but the thoughts of them remain in our hearts forever. Thank you, Sonja and Johnny, for your love, friendship, and support. You will always be in our hearts, no matter where you choose to live.

"In three words I can sum up everything I've learned about life: it goes on."

—Robert Frost

Post Scriptum

When I started to write this book a few months ago, I didn't have an idea as to what lay ahead. The only thing I could rely on was my own faith. I decided to trust my overwhelming feelings (my desires) and do that what seemed inevitable. I know now that because I had the courage to follow my own creative incentive, I am already being abundantly rewarded. Just to clarify my point, I would like to enlighten you with one more anecdote.

As I started to write this book, the first thing that came to my mind was that this was the beginning and the end simultaneously. I did not know the exact meaning of the summoned words until I had finished writing the book, but the sequence of what has happened recently explains everything.

Having been able to deal with my accumulated feelings, I had indeed freed myself from the past. I found home—in myself—never to be lost again. I have also found my thirty-one-year-old US resident alien card with no expiry date on it except the year 1981 imprinted on it, as it had been imprinted on my soul—the year of my adoption. I don't know how I had come to hold on to it for so many years, not knowing the significance. For the first time after coming back to Croatia, I am returning back to the United States, excited that I have gotten rid of the excess burden, astonished that all this while, I was entitled to reside permanently there, from where I fled.

I have, indeed, found home.

Zadar, August 2012